Reflexions about a Cultural and Social Phenomenon: Identity

# STUDIES IN POLITICS, SECURITY AND SOCIETY

Edited by Stanisław Sulowski
Faculty of Political Science and International Studies
University of Warsaw

## VOLUME 36

**PETER LANG**

Jana Popovicsová (ed.)

# Reflexions about a Cultural and Social Phenomenon: Identity

## PETER LANG

**Bibliographic Information published by the Deutsche Nationalbibliothek**
The Deutsche Nationalbibliothek lists this publication in
the Deutsche Nationalbibliografie; detailed bibliographic
data is available in the internet at http://dnb.d-nb.de.

Library of Congress Cataloging-in-Publication Data
A CIP catalog record for this book has been applied for
at the Library of Congress.

This publication was financially supported by the Faculty of Arts, Constantine
the Philosopher University in Nitra

Cover illustration: Courtesy of Benjamin Ben Chaim

ISSN 2199-028X
ISBN 978-3-631-83187-8 (Print)
E-ISBN 978-3-631-84242-3 (E-PDF)
E-ISBN 978-3-631-84243-0 (EPUB)
E-ISBN 978-3-631-84244-7 (MOBI)
DOI 10.3726/b17862

© Peter Lang GmbH
Internationaler Verlag der Wissenschaften
Berlin 2020
All rights reserved.

Peter Lang – Berlin · Bern · Bruxelles · New York · Oxford · Warszawa · Wien

# Table of Contents

# Foreword

The PhD students of the Department of Cultural studies, the Department of Slovak Language and Literature, the Department of Translatology, the Department of Journalism, and the Institute of Literary and Artistic Communication of the Faculty of Constantine the Philosopher University held a PhD Scientific Conference in Nitra on April 27, 2017 entitled "Reflection on Contemporary Cultural and Social Phenomena: Identity."

The aim of the conference was to create a space for postgraduate students to present their scientific activities and confront knowledge from Humanities and several Social Sciences. The publication we are presenting to the public is a collection of several contributions presented at this conference.

The unifying theme of the contributions is *identity*, which is an especially popular issue in contemporary society, culture, and art. The monograph presents many diverse ways of reflecting on identity and the broad interdisciplinary impact of this concept. The authors take the latest theoretical concepts found in culture and social landscapes and apply them to specific areas of their scientific interest.

The authors subject the media system, the cultural sector, and translation concepts to analysis. The authors consider the concept of identity at a national and cultural level, and at the level of gender and personal identity construction in contemporary literature.

The concept of identity is two-fold and both sides are discussed in this collection. On the one hand, identity refers to identicalness, conformity, and sameness. On the other hand, identity refers to something specific and unrepeated that distinguishes individuals or communities from one another.

The publication is primarily intended for professionals and students of humanities, social sciences, and arts.

Barbara Coban

Department of Slovak language and literature, Faculty of
Arts, UKF, Nitra

# Identity in Cyberplace

**Abstract:** Changes in technology often bring about feeling of concern or mistrust. The Internet, which brought not only technological changes but also changes in the public's perception of media, established brand new type of interpersonal communication. However, the concern turned into excitement about new possibilities and fear turned into courage. People started to realize that they are only one click away from doing whatever they want, even breaking the rules, which is nothing out of ordinary either in real life or online one, yet in online world it gets into totally new dimension. New media found its fans mainly among young people; hence, they considered it the most precious information source. Receiving and processing information around people helps them to create their own identity. This is why it is important for information to be selected and used properly. Internet ethics is an essential point of life standard and it influences the whole society. Even in the virtual world, it is important to be considerate and keep one's dignity as Internet ethics and ethics in general have been emphasized a lot in recent years.

**Keywords:** Internet, ethics, unethical, identity, cyberspace, cyberbullying.

## Internet and Cyberspace / Electronic Media

Despite initial skepticism, the Internet has become a mass medium which influences the lives of many people. The Internet is a dynamic, broadscale medium, and the main drive behind the information boom. It serves as a constant source of information and in many instances it has served as a replacement for existing media (the press, radio, television). The Internet may even be a catalyst in a global communication revolution, since online communication often replaces "real life" communication. There is no doubt that Internet as a medium is here to stay and that its impact on current lifestyle will be lasting. Having said that, the Internet is not all bad. Technology helps people save time, because it makes processes in every field shorter, hence, the whole systems becomes more efficient. The

Internet provides people with easily accessible information and offers the advantage of sending and receiving a large amount of data. Apart from a new economic prosperity and more efficient interpersonal interaction, the Internet also leads society to "having more flexible identities than we had before, which brings new dimensions into our lives" Dreyfus (2001, p. 2).

One can look at the Internet from various perspectives. The Internet may be called "the network of networks," which represents the great infrastructure that connects computer and data networks of commercial, non-commercial, governmental, and military institutions with schools, academic organizations, and also individuals. From technical point of view, it may be considered a net of complex operations that enable millions of Internet users to get online. *Slovník mediální komunikace* [Dictionary of Media Communication] (2004, p. 94) defines the Internet as a "world-wide computer network made out of various bigger and smaller computer networks using TCP/IP (Transmission Control over Internet Protocol) for digital data transmission. Internet is hierarchically organized; the small networks are part of bigger ones, whilst the greatest operators provide global connection."

We may also generally say that the Internet is not only a technical invention and an information channel but also a medium of mass communication. The Internet clearly fulfils the basic functions of media. It is informative, entertaining, educational, and promotional, among other attributes. It is publicly accessible and practically limitless. One of Internet's advantages is its ability to interact with others around the world and receive feedback almost immediately. Right after having read an article or having watched a video, Internet users are able to respond and express their opinions. Online forums and email open up the possibility of quick and limitless feedback. The ease and speed of feedback reduces boundaries between the author and the recipient, giving space for informal discussion. It has been said that "especially in new media, it is reflected in recipient's contribution in creating the final product by choosing from the offer, combining different notifications, even deciding about its final form (*Slovník*, p. 94)."

Even though the Internet is made up of a combination of various media features, it has its own specific characteristics. Internet users have access to a large amount of information, yet they may select information themselves. This may be called "Internet freedom." In "traditional" media, one only receives the given, limited content, whereas the Internet offers a broad range of information, which contributes to one's feeling of freedom and liberation from manipulative regulations of superior societies or censorship. The accessibility the internet offers eliminates the common feeling of subordination and provides a kind of equality between users. Not only has it become a working tool but also a point of interest for various business activities. The Internet has become something that provides working opportunities to more and more users, such as creation of online content or development of applications. It is also a place with various online shops, news, books or audio-visual works. Moreover, the Internet is a perfect place for pop culture to spread, and today it has an irreplaceable place in our society. It is thanks to the Internet that information society emerged.

"Medium is the Message," declares McLuhan, the "father" of the electronic age. The electronic ages have brought many advantages and disadvantages. McLuhan believes one becomes what one continually sees. In his studies, McLuhan examines the outline of humanity, which, when given the chance over time, creates technology and inevitable tries to understand itself. He considers media a legacy. McLuhan holds that every type of media contains different medium, which is why one can discuss strong and intense effects of each medium, or rather media as a whole. He divides media into two categories according to their effect on the audience: hot (radio, movie, book) and cold (telephone, television, speech, discussion). The supposed "hot" media are meant to be explosive, specialized, and individualizing; while the "cold" media are social, inner, and require participation. The coldest medium, according to McLuhan, is television.

Various scientific disciplines, including psychology, sociology, physics, chemistry, and computer technology use media. These disciplines consider media as something that channels the information from creator to recipient by means of various signals and codes. The philosophy of mass media is a new philosophic discipline[1] that focuses on two areas: philosophical

---

1 Gažová claims that mass media philosophy is "a discipline that analyses connections and relations between technical, symbolic, semantic and sensory aspect of human communication and records the changes that appear with the arrival of new technologies" (2003. p. 9).

research of media and the philosophy of communication. It concentrates on four types of media: speech, writing, print, and electronic media. Jean Lohisse (2003, p. 8) also includes epochs alongside the media types: way of speaking, epoch of speaking; writing, writing epoch; print, mass epoch, and electronic media; epoch without a shape.

The most dominant medium in the era of speaking is the human language. One that is made up of not only auditory components but also by the visual and kinetic ones. Language has a crucial impact on the creation of a collective mentality. In the writing epoch, we come across the opinion that the writing system was a powerful tool leading to externalization and fixation on people's thoughts and words. The basic writing characteristics is a linear segmentation of characters which influences the collective mentality and social organization. The mass media epoch starts with the invention of printing in 1455. Printing was already considered an important information medium back in the fifteenth century. Therefore, 150 years later, after the invention of printing, the era gave rise to the periodic press, which aimed mainly at reaching bigger groups of society, the masses. However, the spread of printing was conditioned by people's literacy.

The Internet is currently the fastest developing and publicly shared tool, being a leading medium in the "epoch without a shape." Its informative and educational possibilities are nearly limitless whilst its usage is universal. It enables us not only to receive information and education, but also provides an opportunity for users to participate in information exchange and data presentation. The information epoch began in the second half of the twentieth century and goes hand in hand with the development of information technologies.

The ability to take in mass information is a rather powerful tool in modern society. One's wealth, status, and influence all depend on one's ability to processes information. If some media entity possesses information it wants to share, it is up to the developers of that media entity to decide how exactly they will share the content with the desired target group. Concerning this topic, Jirák and Köpplová (2003, p. 11) claim that "media enters one's personal life and, to a great extent, brings along a public dimension shared with others. Meanwhile, media shapes the life of society and brings in many, rather intimate, features. Public and common sphere decide upon the media's conduction, whilst influencing itself by this dynamic interaction. Media also offer numerous life interpretations that constantly repeat themselves, provide us with information about values, attitudes, opinions which are, or because of media communication seem to be, shared with others." Understanding and interpreting information that appears in media is a complicated process that requires a certain degree of education and the ability to provide one's own argument and defend them. It goes without saying that media make a great impact on people, their behavior, lifestyle, and opinions.

## Social Networks

Nowadays, media may be divided into two groups; the new and the old. Printing, radio, and television are now considered "old." The question as to what exactly belongs to "new" media is problematic. Čermák weighs in on the problem of "new" media stating: "which media are new, and which are old? When will current 'new media' stop being new and when will newer ones appear and replace them? Although, it is only a word play, it shows how helpless we are when it comes to defining new media" (2009, p. 7). The world and technology are constantly developing. The twentieth century radio and television once belonged to new media, and likewise in the 1990s, the Internet was considered new media. Irena Reifová (2004, p. 134) considers new media a means of communication that uses computer technologies for information transmission and storage. Every technological development brings along both advantages and disadvantages. Advantages of the Internet are speed, responsiveness, and reach. However, the risk of addiction is greater in this case than in the case of printed newspapers, but it is yet the greatest disadvantage. The reason for it is easy Internet access in nearly every household. David Šmahel (2003) presents the Internet as a complex reflection of society and mankind, a reflection of that shows us who we really are.

Social media has become the latest world sensation. The terms Facebook, Instagram, Twitter, vlog, follower, like, share, post, etc. are all around us. At its core, social media is a mean of online communication with both active creators of content and passive recipients (Štefančíková, 2006, p. 119). In a simplified way, social media is a technology for sharing and communicating, whilst, when it comes to social networks, we speak of "means of communication." Initially, this communication was via email, chat rooms, later, there were blogs, Skype (online chat using web camera), and today there is Facebook – used mainly for sharing opinions, Instagram – for sharing photos or YouTube where one may share their videos with various content.

Nowadays, content crosses the border between professional and amateur. According to Scott (2010), social media of today differs from the classic ones mainly in the content made by a regular Internet user. In simple terms, social network is a structure of formal and informal relations, independent of each other, which provide different forms of social services operating in certain locality. In the online world, a social network represents a system that allows Internet users make, build, and keep online contacts among friends, relatives, and often strangers as well. The beginning of the social network dates back to 1985. However, social network was not successful at the time as the Internet was not as easily accessible, and thus not as popular among the masses as it is now. The most successful social network has been Facebook, created in 2004 by Mark Zuckerberg. No other social network has been able to gain the same amount of success as Facebook. Slovakia also tried to create its own network, the best known was pokec.sk. Our contemporary and fast paced world often prefers online conversation over face to face interactions, which is reflected online, where users connected via social networks may connect at any time and any place.

Social networks may be divided into three categories: 1. Informative – users search for general information about a topic they are interested in and for communities that discuss such topics; 2. Professional – based on professional relations between employer and employee or between company and job applicant; 3. Educational – such as Moodle, which by means of educational courses connects people who are interested in a certain topic or study it. They may work together, conduct research, and consult teachers.

## Ethics and Netiquette

The term "ethics" is generally understood as a philosophical discipline that deals with the study of morality. Aristotle was one of the first who started using the term ethics relating it not only to learning about morality but also morality itself. (Remišová, Gažová, 2003, p. 7) Moral rules are inevitable, not only for well-based society but also for individuals. Ethics is not really directive, it does not present any commands, restrictions or strict normative rules. Ethics is more of a manual that describes how to behave and determines the borders of good and evil. Ethics may be understood as a philosophical and ideational system. However, it is necessary to highlight the fact that the foundation of ethical behavior in one country may be unacceptable in a different country, and vice versa. Ethical rules may be influenced by external factors such as cultural and social environments. Something that was considered absolutely unethical years ago could nowadays be considered ethically appropriate. Likewise, anything that is a moral misstep today may be a common practice in the future. Naturally, ethics has been adapting to the perception of values that may change and twist over the years. Ethics help us to learn what kind of attitude we should choose in real life. It instructs us what we should do in particular situations, how to behave, and what to consider a right behavior (Remišová, Gažová, 2003, pp. 7–8).

Media ethics is applied ethics that deals with media of all kinds, forms, and levels. Media ethics is the study of morality and the development of ethics in the media sphere. It is a theoretical and practical base for media production aligned to certain values that occur in the public interest and the humanity interest (Remišová, 2010, pp. 21–22). Within the scale of moral rules applied to the media sphere, each type of media is defined by different characteristic features. Fobelová (2005, p. 97) refers to Klaus Wigerling in her book. Klaus Wigerling defines the area of media ethics in three points: 1) media ethics studies the relationship between media expression and human behavior, 2) media ethics tries to define how much is media responsible for behavior, 3) it tries to apply ethics order into the area of media.

The information presented in the media has a strong impact on consumers. It is not uncommon for someone to see something in media and decide that the content is right and trustworthy, just because it has been published, which ultimately transforms our behavior. Ethical character of content is very important, because of the impact it has on human action and behavior.

Technological progress and the growth of Internet made it necessary to create a list of proper behaviors for Internet use, which are commonly called Netiquette (Network Etiquette). This is confirmed by the document RSC 1855 Netiquette Guidelines (1995) which contains recommendations as to how Internet users should behave online. In ordinary life, parents teach children how to behave nicely toward the others, but communication on the Internet often lacks rule, therefore, the following words should always be on our minds: "we are equal in the online world and any unethical practices used against anyone may be applied against ourselves in the same way. However, apparent anonymity of a computer terminal causes that we forget about it to the point that we allow ourselves to do things which we would never do in direct communication (vulgarisms, lying, cheating etc.)" (Poláková, 2006, p. 105). It is up to every user as to how they will decide to behave in relation to other users, so it makes sense for users to think that they have license to do or say anything online. First, it is necessary to take caution when sharing anything online and really consider what we share on the Internet.

Netiquette may be understood as a kind of agreement between participants of the communication on the electronic network. The official rules of netiquette are listed in the publication of Request for Comments (RSC 1855). It is a 20–page long document divided into three main sections that delineate the three main types of netiquette. The first regards one-on-one communication or interactions between individuals like e-mail and chat. The basis of this section is mainly to regulate sent messages and the principles of copyrights. Moreover, the first section warns against drawing conclusions too quickly, urging users to give the addressee time to react to an e-mail, because it may happen that the addressee does not spend a lot of time on the Internet. Most importantly, this section encourages good behavior, polite communication and avoiding arguments.

The second section is directed toward interactions between individuals among bigger groups of people, such as group e-mail messages and information services including World Wide Web etc. In this section, there is a warning that the opinion of the author of the e-mail message does not automatically have to be the opinion of the whole company. It also emphasizes the importance of "knowing your audience." With regard to mass email blasts, this section encourages users to make sure that the information included is relevant to the addressees and advises the users to give recipients the option of unsubscribing in case they are no longer interested in receiving e-mails.

The last section covers ethics for administrators of websites. According to the guidelines, website administrators should give visitors access to the website's basic rules, frequently asked questions, and information stressing what of the website's content may and may not be copied. It is also important to explain what happens with any information that the website requests as a part of registration. Finally, administrators should be aware of Internet viruses that have the potential to harm the website's visitors. This document is primarily dedicated to administrators who are in charge of newsletters or those who take care of websites. It does not give information for regular users of the Internet.

Basic rules for the common Internet user are summarized in the book *Netiquette* by Virginia Shea (1994). In her books, Shea mainly stresses the importance of the rules of netiquette and how these rules are necessary especially in today's climate when Internet communication has become a part of almost everyone's ordinary lives. These especially apply especially to those users who often forget that even though they are communicating in online space and cannot see and be in the presence of those they are talking to, they are nevertheless communicating with real people. This is why Shea introduces 10 basic principles for Internet behavior.

## Rule 1: "Think about the human."

Shea is urging us to remember that there is a real person on the other side of our comment. It does not matter if it is an e-mail or a chat message, it is really easy for messages to be misinterpreted, because users cannot see the facial expression or gestures of the others. Moreover, we cannot hear the tone of voice. The anonymity may lead users to forget that he or she is talking to a real person. This is especially dangerous when he or she has never met the person before and would not have met them if it was not for the Internet. At such a time, users should ask themselves: "Would I say this to the person's face?" It is a good practice to read the message once again before you send it, and if the answer is "no," try to rewrite it. Another reason why users should be aware of etiquette on the Internet is the fact that Internet communication is a kind of communication that can be saved by users in screenshots. Screenshots and print screens may be shared anywhere without the original user's consent.

## Rule 2: "Adhere to the same standards of behavior online that you follow in real life."

In person, people follow laws and rules, not only because of how they have been raised, but also because they are afraid of consequences of breaking them. Online, people forget that a real person will receive their comments. They think that the rules of ethics do not have to be followed as strictly as offline.

## Rule 3: "Know where you are in cyberspace."

Users must remember that what is acceptable in one user community, might be a faux pass in another. For example, gossiping in the Facebook group of fans of a television series is normal, but spreading unverified information in a group chat of journalists would be inappropriate. Before posting to a new online community, it is important to "look around." New users are invited to read the rules, observe how the members communicate with each other and how they behave. Once acquainted, a user may then join the communication is an appropriate manner.

## Rule 4: "Respect other people's time and bandwidth."

If you are working on a project or are dealing with a conflict, it is easy to forget that this particular problem is likely not the center of another user's attention. In cases like these, do not wait for an automatic, fast response. Moreover, try to limit the length of posts in discussion groups so that readers do not have to parse through a lot of information before reaching the main point. If you send group e-mails, make sure all of the information included is necessary for the reader to know.

## Rule 5: "Make yourself look good online."

*Use your anonymity.* The "other side" does not see you most of the time, thus they cannot judge you or create any opinion that would be based on anything else than the style of your writing. Good spelling may help to improve your online. *Know what you are talking about and make sense –* verify facts before you publish them online, because an effect similar to Chinese whispers may occur. Wrong information spreads quickly and when it comes back to you, chances are that you will not recognize what you yourself once wrote. Write meaningfully and try to limit long words. *Do not initiate conflicts.* Nowadays, this is one of the most important (if not the most important) rule. Do not use offensive language and do not initiate any fights just because you can. Conflicts are very common in online discussions, either on Facebook or in the comment section of various websites. Avoid swearing, using euphemisms or "censored versions."

*Share expert knowledge.* The power of the Internet is in the number of people who share. People ask questions on online forums to find a person is knowledgeable on a topic. If you are knowledgeable on a certain topic, do not be afraid to share that knowledge. If a few of knowledgeable people offer useful information, the knowledge of the whole group increases. On the other hand, if you have ever had an interesting question and have been given a useful answer, share it with others. Along the same lines, if you have ever done research on a subject that people might find interesting, sum up the results of the research in an article or an online post.

## Rule 7. "Help keep 'flame wars' under control."

The term "flaming" in the context of online discussion, is an online exchange that has a tendency to overstep the boundary between beneficial exchange of opinions and conflict. "Flaming" is usually seen in discussion forums or in the comment section of websites. Netiquette does not prohibit flaming itself but warns against it only when it triggers offensive language and insults. The signs of a flame war are a big increase in posts or comments that leads to a situation when, even those who are not participating in the fights, get spammed. A flame war is characterized by an unusual purpose. The goal is not to convince the opponent, but rather to defeat him by making him angry. The "flames" are intentionally unfriendly and offensive words toward the opponent. Flame wars grow bigger with each reaction. In cases like these, "troll," often enter the conversation. "Trolls" are known for provoking a "flame war" with an opinion that has little to nothing to do with the topic at hand.

## Rule 8. "Respect people's privacy."

It is important not to share the e-mails of others without their approval. Sharing an email without asking first may result in the original sender receiving unwanted messages from strangers or spam mail. Moreover, most importantly, do not read the messages and e-mails of other people.

## Rule 9. "Do not abuse your power."

There are many administrators of various web domains who have access to the sensitive information of users. It is important not misuse this power. Administrators should never read user's private correspondences.

## Rule10. "Be forgiving of other people's mistakes."

This final point applies mainly to correcting mistakes and grammar of others. It is normal for people to make mistakes and it is wrong to constantly correct these mistakes. If you feel need to point a certain mistake out, do it briefly and do not be arrogant. Inappropriate correction of grammar is actually a violation of proper netiquette (source 1).

The Internet brings many threats. Every social network encourages its visitors to publish their personal information. With the arrival of Facebook, there have been instances when personal information was both mistakenly and voluntarily leaked. Many people do not have any idea who can see their profile on Facebook or any other social media. Users often share some of their most intimate information. Information that we publish on the network is offered to all of the users, whether users like it or not. Privacy is at stake. Moral and social boundaries among groups are vanishing. However, on the other hand, the Internet may be useful when conducting a job search, because employers often try to search for any information about potential employee on the social networks.

By publishing personal information, users are taking a risk that their information might fall into the wrong hands. It is not uncommon for a private image to be turned into a joke and spread among people who were not supposed to see it. For instance, users may publish sensitive photos of someone to a social network and tag the person in that photo with their name. It is possible to delete the photo, but in the meantime, the photo could be seen by many people. Moreover, the photo could even be downloaded and saved sooner than the tagged person sees it and requests its removal. Not only Facebook, but also the thousands of other applications that we use currently or have used in the past have access to our data. Furthermore, deleting one's data is not an effective remedy because these applications always archive all of the data ever imputed in order to create statistics, databases, and to aid in marketing. These things add to the loss of user privacy, not only on social networks, but also on the Internet at large. Current research shows that 15 % of all users of these portals do not keep private information secret at all, 24 % of them use the same password on multiple websites, 19 % of users of social networks looks for information about their old love (this number increases to 39 % among 25–34 years old). One out of three users use the media outlet to search for information about his boss, colleague, or job seeker (source 2).

## Identity and Cyberplace Identity

Identity has been a subject of interest for many scientists and disciplines for over 60 years. The notion of identity was discussed in Sigmund Freud's conceptions, but the term was actually used for the first time by E. R. Hilgard. Hilgard defined identity as a center of interest for psychology experts in his speech at the American Psychological Association in Denver in 1949 and declared it one of the key topics of modern psychology. Later, the concept of identity was examined in greater detail by psychoanalyst E. H. Erikson.

The topic of identity is still highly discussed. The Dictionary of Psychological Concepts (2009) defines identity as "experiencing and real-izing yourself, its uniqueness and its differences from others." Sociology and social psychology define identity as a set of attributes, values, goals, tastes, and convictions that make a person unique in their eyes and in the eyes of others (Duffková et al., 2008, p. 105). Hajko speaks of iden-tity as both a way of survival while honoring one's uniqueness and as the principle of what makes one different from the others (2005, p. 33). In general, identity is the relationship between two or more entities that agree in all the qualities. On a deeper level, identity is also the perception of oneself and involves the realization of identity within the environment.

My identity makes me who I am, it is my essence. In order for a man to become a credible human being, he must find himself, his identity. Today, in the twenty-first century, there is a great challenge to "be yourself." The process of becoming aware of identity requires interaction with the outside world. We need to socialize and talk to develop our social identity. Acquiring identity is a never-ending process. We acquire it subjectively and acquire it in relation to individual events. One's ability to maintain their own identity stultifies globalization and multicultural tendencies and societal changes.

Virtual representation is a cluster of ordered data or information that is routinely shared in the Internet environment. These things include name / nickname,[2] history, and social status. Users then render their thinking and feelings to shape their virtual representation. Some virtual identities may overlap with the representation of the person, but this is not to be considered equivalent to the psychological definition of identity. Online identity allows users to show and share those parts of their identity that are not usually shared in the real world. Sometimes, virtual identity does not match the "real" one. Virtual identity may often be an attempt to impress others (Ševčíková – Šmahel, 2010, p. 114). Identity building is a complex psychological process and it is primarily a topic for psychology and sociology. However, virtual identity grows in the virtual space. Divinová and Šmahel (2010, p. 126) point to the feature of cyberspace that distinguishes social networks from previous communication systems (for example from chat): the identity that social network users present is often identical to their real identity.

Virtual identity may be similar, or identical to one's real identity, but it may also be different. Oftentimes, online users use the Internet to experiment with their identity. These experiments are made possible because of the anonymity of the Internet. There are two main ways to perceive the identity. There is the traditional one and the postmodern. Traditionally, identity was considered to be relatively stable and established in the early years of life, while the postmodern concept claims that identity is pluralistic, dynamic, and asserts that every individual may have more identities (Fuchs, 2008, p. 321).

---

2   Šmahel uses "nick."

The Internet is an environment of absent of barriers. It gives users a place to overcome shyness and do away with rules and taboos. In the virtual world, people often say and do what they probably would do in the real world. Some are kind and generous. Others attack through vulgarisms, anger, hatred, in extreme cases, we may come across violence or pornography.

## Cyberbullying

Inevitably, every human activity brings about both only positives and negative consequences. The Internet is a true proof of this fact. Inappropriate behavior is part of daily lives and the Internet is only a new mean of its manifestation. Anyone may be an aggressor, a victim, and a quiet bystander. With regards to bullying, there are lighter forms that we encounter commonly, and more difficult forms that may lead to depression, psychological disorders, or even suicide.

The development of the Internet brought about a new kind of bullying called cyberbullying. Cyberbullying is a form of bullying that uses technology such as a computer, or mobile phone. Cyberbullying takes place in the virtual space using various services and tools such as email, IM (instant messenger – Skype, ICQ), chat, forums, social networks, photo and video publishing sites, blogs, SMS messages, phone calls (Source 3).

New forms of communication have allowed cyberbullying to become a permanent place in current society. Oftentimes, aggressors are those who do not succeed at bullying in real life and rely on the anonymity of the cyberspace to given them courage. According to Bill Belsey, "cyberbullying involves the use of information and communication technologies to support the deliberate, repeated, and hostile behavior by an individual or group, which is intended to harm others" (Source 4).

It might seem that cyberbullying cannot do much harm, but the truth is opposite. The biggest difference between bullying and cyberbullying lies in anonymity. While "classical" bullying requires the aggressor and the victim to meet personally, in the case of cyberbullying, victims often do not know who is hiding behind the harassment. The power of anonymity intensifies aggressive behavior, because the aggressor acts as if they were unattainable and were no longer afraid of punishment since there is no face-to-face contact. The cyberspace in general often lacks sensitivity and empathy, which allows aggressors to increase their aggression without consequence since users do not take cyberbullying seriously. Aggressors often do not realize their behavior, but victims are still distraught as they cannot defend themselves and many times do not know where the attack is coming from.

Zasepa (2002) points out to Internet users claiming that those who are weaker and lazier in offline life often feel more powerful in online contact and tend to share information that only they know. This openness may be misused by the aggressor. In "classical" bullying, it is assumed that a physically fitter person bullies an outsider, while in cyberbullying roles may be swapped. Cyberbullying is non-standard in many ways. It does not have the classical visible signs of bullying; therefore, it usually lasts until a specific problem or danger reveals. It also spreads fast (Kovářová, 2009, p. 17).

There are many of forms of cyberbullying. Cyberbullying includes insulting, threatening or sending harassing emails. The lightest form of cyberbullying is spam or junk mail. Worse forms are accompanied by threats. It is best not to respond to these messages, because the aggressor is motivated only by the victim's reaction and the caused fear. E-mail services offer a message filter feature that can block messages from specific users. However, if the aggressor wants to continue bullying, it is possible to continue the harassment by sending mail from another account or using another means.

Bullying is also common through chats or in chat rooms. Chats and chat rooms are forms of real-time communication, which can make the victim feel as if they were in greater danger. Cyberbullying in chat rooms may take many forms. Moreover, bullying may consist in public defamation, "the spreading of gossip, sharing personal information, or exclusion from the group. It is not uncommon for aggressors to begin their cyberbullying by being friendly toward their victims to build trust before the abuse begins. Chat rooms are also one of the most common means for attackers' predators to initiate personal meetings with adolescents. For this reason, it is important for parents to caution children against strangers on the Internet. It is specifically important to warn that not everything on the Internet is credible. One can never know who may be hiding under a nickname. For instance, it is possible that the supposed 15-year-old boy is actually a 50-year-old man.

Social media presents users with a high potential risk for many kinds of abuse. Users often publish their name and real personal information such as address, school or telephone number. Personal information and private posts, such as photos or videos, are easy for abusers to misuse. Users whose information is publicly published are especially easy targets. Publishing photos or videos on the Internet is common, but if these posts get into the wrong hands, they may spread uncontrollably. Usually, people become victims of cyberbullying, because their password gets stolen. Most of the time, the attacker impersonates the victim and posts inappropriate messages in the victim's name or sends out harassing messages to the victim's friends. With this stolen identity, attackers spread untrue or embarrassing information.

The causes of bullying are always different. Behavior of some aggressors is triggered by anger or hatred. In one-time bullying, people usually attack out of a fit of rage and are simply taking their feelings out on someone who is weaker. In cases like these, after the anger dissolves, the aggressive reactions stop, and cyberbullying is over. In lighter cases of bullying, the attackers often do not consider their attacks as bullying but only as "harmless fun." These aggressors do not know the boundary between joking, and unpleasant mockery which makes its victim suffer. When the bullying continues for a very long time, the consequences for the victim's psychological health are much more serious. A bullied child may suffer long-term psychological, self-confidence problems, and various disorders.

Furthermore, there are cases of persistent stalking caused by unrequited love when an individual cannot bare the separation or rejection. The question of what to do about cyberbullying has been discussed in several studies, and there are many websites on the Internet that offer help to victims. Helplines and tutorials advise children and adults how to proceed. The big problem is that children are often afraid to tell their parents about them being victims of cyberbullying, because often the parent's most common solution is to ban the child from using the Internet. Another reason could be that children are embarrassed about the content of the messages or the information published, so they hide in fear until the situation resolves.

Ten Commandments for Schoolchildren:

1. Do not forget: A careful Internet user is an intelligent user. 2. Do not give your address or your phone number to anybody. You do not know who is hiding behind the screen. 3. Do not send your photos to anyone and do not share your age. 4. Keep the password of your e-mail secret. Do not give it to anyone, even friends. 5. Never respond to rude, abusive, or vulgar emails. 6. Do not agree to a meeting through the Internet without consulting a parent first. 7. If any picture or e-mail shocks you, leave the website immediately. 8. Tell an adult if the Internet frightens or embarrasses you. 9. Beware of online viruses. Do not open a message attachment that was delivered from an unknown address. 10. Do not trust everything you read on the Internet (Source 5).

Cyberbullying affects victims psychologically, but if it does not stop and if it is pushed to the extreme, it may lead to assault or even bodily harm. According to Botík and Jánošová (2011, p. 126), cyberbullying "based on psychological form of aggression is even more dangerous than in its physical form." In physical bullying, there are spectators who sometimes interfere, but that would be very rare in a cyberbullying situation. If there are any spectators at all, they generally consider themselves to be impartial observers and consider bullying only as fun and games. Many Internet users lack compassion and do not take internet harassment seriously. If we would become victims of cyberbullying, we would quickly understand that cyberbullying should not be taken lightly, especially when it comes to children who are still emotionally fragile and are not capable of handling a situation like this.

## Conclusions

Today's electronic age is often considered highly independent. People tend to avoid direct communication and prefer communication via the Internet. Social networks are the most common since they allow users to communicate with people regardless of time, place, age, etc. Users communicate with people they know and trust, and strangers. The virtual world is based upon reality and in a way, is a subset of it. The real world offers us the same possibilities as the virtual world, although these possibilities come with certain difficulties. In the virtual world, the possibilities at our fingertips are nearly limitless and there are few boundaries to creating one's own identity. To conclude, it is necessary to be cautious when using the Internet because what is happening on social networks and in virtual world as a whole may or may not have anything to do with reality.

## References:

BOTÍK, M. – JÁNOŠOVÁ, D.: Kyberšikana ako aktuálny problém. In: *Limity mediálnej Internetovej komunikácie – Megatrendy a médiá* Trnava: UCM FMK, 2011, pp. 117–129. ISBN 978-80-8105-254-5.

ČERMÁK, M.: Nová média. Úvod a stručná historie. In: *Žurnalistika v informační společnosti: digitalizace a Internetizace žurnalistiky*. 1. vyd. Praha: Karolinum, 2009, pp. 7–42. ISBN 978-80-246-1684-1.

DREYFUS, H.: On the Internet. London: Taylor & Francis Group, 2001, p. 145. ISBN 97811-3458-650-9.

DUFFKOVÁ, J. – URBAN, L. – DUBSKÝ, J.: Sociologie životního stylu. Plzeň: Vydavatelství a nakladatelství Aleš Čeněk, 2008, p. 237. ISBN 978-80-7380-123-6.

FOBELOVÁ, D.: Aplikované etiky v kontextoch súčasnosti. Banská Bystrica: Univerzita Mateja Bela, 2005, p. 112. ISBN 80-8083-141-6.

FUCHS, CH.: Internet and society: social theory in the information age. New York: Routledge, 2008, 398 p. ISBN 978–0–415–96132–5.

GAŽOVÁ, V.: Filozofia médií. In: *Médiá na prahu tretieho tisícročia. Človek v sieti mediálnej recepcie*. Trnava: FMK UCM, 2003, pp. 9–22. ISBN 80-89034-34-9.

HAJKO, D.: Globalizácia a kultúrna identita. Nitra: Univerzita Konštantína Filozofa v Nitre, Nitra, 2005, p. 128. ISBN 80-8050-913-1.

JIRÁK, J. – KÖPPLOVÁ, B.: Médiá a spoločnosť. 2. vyd. Praha: Portál, 2003. p. 208. ISBN 80-7178-697-7.

KOVÁŘOVÁ, V. a kol.: Kyberšikana a její prevence – příručka pro učitele. Plzeň: DRAGON PRESS, 2009. p. 108. ISBN 978-80-86961-78-1.

LOHISSE, J.: Komunikační systémy. Praha: Karolinum, 2003, p. 198. ISBN 80-246-0301-2.

POLÁKOVÁ, E.: Mediálne kompetencie. Úvod do problematiky mediálnych kompetencií. Zväzok I. Trnava: FMK UCM Trnava, 2006, 146 p. ISBN 978–80–89528–02–8.

REIFOVÁ, I.: Slovník mediální komunikace. Praha: Portál, 2004, 328 p. ISBN 80–71789–26–7.

REMIŠOVÁ, A. – GAŽOVÁ, V.: Vybrané kapitoly z etiky a kulturológie. 2. doplnené vydanie. Trnava: UCM – FMK, 2003, p. 144. ISBN 80-8934-55-1.

REMIŠOVÁ, A.: Etika médií. Bratislava: Kaligram, 2010, p. 291. ISBN 978-80-8101-3768.

SHEA,V.: Netiquette. Albion Books: New York. 1994, p. 154. ISBN: 9780963702517.

ŠEVČÍKOVÁ, A. – ŠMAHEL, D.: Konstrukce virtuální identity u dospívajících uţivatelů Internetu. In: TYRLÍK, M. – MACEK, P. – ŠIRŮČEK, J. *Sebepojetí a identita v adolescenci: sociální a kulturní kontext*. 1. vyd. Brno: Masarykova univerzita, 2010, p. 144. ISBN 978-80-210-5107-2.

ŠMAHEL, D.: *Psychologie a Internet: děti dospělými, dospělí dětmi*. Praha: Triton, 2003, p. 158. ISBN 80-7254-360-1.

ŠTEFANČÍKOVÁ, A.: Kyberkultúra a komunikácia. In: *Médiá na prahu tretieho tisícročia: súčasný stav mediálnej kultúry*. Trnava: FMK UCM, 2006, p. 119. ISBN 8089220-07-X

ZASĘPA, T.: Média v čase globalizácie. Bratislava: LÚČ, 2002, p. 425. ISBN 80-7114387-1.

## Online Sources:

Source 1: RSC 1885: *Netiquette Guidelines* [online]. [cit. 2019-02-24]. Retrieved from: https://www.ietf.org/rfc/rfc1855.txt.

Source 2: GUJBEROVÁ, M.: *Nebezpečenstvá sociálnych sietí*. [online]. 2009. [cit. 2019-02-24]. Retrieved from: http://gujbi.blog.matfyz.sk/p14062–nebezpecenstva-socialnych-sieti.

Source 3: eSlovensko o.z.: *Kyberšikanovanie*. [online]. [cit. 2019-02-24]. Retrieved from: http://www.zodpovedne.sk/kapitola2.php?kat=kybersikanovanie.

Source 4: BELSEY, B.: *The World's First Definition of "Cyberbullying."* [online]. [cit. 2019–]. Retrieved from: http://www.cyberbullying.ca/.

Source 5: *Projekt Bezpečný Internet dětem*. [online]. [cit. 2019–02–24]. *Dostupné na Internete*: https://www.nasedite.cz/kampan/bezpecny-Internet-detem-67/.

Zuzana Jánošíková

Department of English Language and Literature, Faculty of
Education, Trnava Univeristy in Trnava

# Identity and the Intercultural Journey of a Translation

**Abstract:** This paper maps out the concept and forms of identity within the field of translation. Considering the intercultural nature of translation, this contribution deals with identity in its selected forms as it contributes to creating translation as a final product. It discussed the issue of identity reflected in a text, a subject of a translator, reader, and also original and target contexts. Furthermore, it briefly analyzes one of the most significant parts of the translation process, i.e. the subjective and objective nature of translating in combination with the blending of these two dimensions in the form of interpretation.

**Keywords:** Translation, identity, interpretation, context, translator, interculturality.

## Introduction or Thinking on Identity in Terms of Translation (Studies)

The essence of any translation activity is derived from the need of transferring a text – or whatever its form may be – from a source to a target language, thus creating a new text (or any other product) as a final product of this translation process. One might claim that it is necessary to add that translation is more than just a linguistic operation as it is also a transfer from one culture to another. Moreover, we may also think about translation as a form of transfer of any information or identity from one recipient to another.

What do all of these categories have in common? They all have their own identity. Is it therefore important to discuss the issue of identity within the field of translation studies? We believe that the very nature of the act of translation deals with this problem in various forms. Some of them will be addressed in this contribution. We suppose it is quite clear that the question of identity may be nowadays considered one of the most frequently

discussed matters. Moreover, when we mention the blending of the identities, languages, cultures, traditions, and aesthetic qualities, we basically
refer to the main principle of translation. Therefore, in this paper, we have
decided to discuss selected forms of identity as reflected within the translation studies research, focusing on the translation process and its specifics.

## Identity of Translation, Translation of Identity

As we mentioned in the beginning, the concept of identity belongs perhaps
to one of the most frequently discussed issues. This means there is a variety
of approaches, theories, definitions, and characteristics related to this
term. However, we understand it here simply as the essence of someone or
something, as a sum of the characteristics of a person or a thing.

The center of our attention will be focused on three main topics: the
identity of a text (bearing in mind that this text is just an example of
any other form of information entering the translation process); a context (original and target) and its possible specifics (focusing mainly on the
selected external factors, such as possible cultural, historical, political or
other conditions determining the process), and the identity related to a
human aspect in translation (especially in the form of translator).

First of all, it is necessary to realize that these forms of identity do
not exist in a vacuum. They co-exist and are influenced by both each
other and a great spectrum of other factors that we will try to blend
into the problematics to see how they basically "shape" these identities.
When thinking about translation process, one cannot avoid seeing these
"identities" in their intercultural nature. In fact, translation as a creative
activity may be placed between two sometimes very different contexts,
cultures, countries, systems of traditions, literary systems, customs, values,
languages etc. It is precisely the confrontation of these specifics that makes
it so unique each time. In general, transferring one identity from the original to the target context includes a great variety of processes, phases, and
stages, which lead to the final product. However simple this might seem,
it is not.

The whole range of identities that participate in creating the final
product in the form of a translation includes a lot more. It is necessary to
take into consideration a number of things. First of all, it is important to

consider the specifics, which we believe form and shape the identities of many other factors such as authors. We include authors not only because of the wider social, political, historical context but also because of possible important biographical features. We will also consider readers, since we are convinced that they are one of the most significant factors for the decision-making process during translation. Nevertheless, it is possible that this category will differ in original and target contexts. We also consider editors reviewers, as they are both representatives of various forms of preferred or favored practices within a certain publishing house or wider context. Therefore, although our aim is to focus more on the selected ones, it is impossible to embrace the problematics of translation in its complexity without at least mentioning briefly also these aspects through examining the whole process.

## Intercultural Aspect of Translation

Translation acquires its intercultural dimension with the process of transferring text from one cultural context to another, as its intercultural nature is in confrontation of these two cultures. Therefore, it is the intercultural communication that marks the actual and real essence of translation. Průcha (2010) refers to this intercultural communication as one of the phenomena arising as a result of rapid and world-wide development of civilization. Průcha further classifies this phenomenon as, on the one hand, positive in terms of mutual familiarization among cultures, nations and countries and cooperation of various people, nations and cultures and on the other hand, he points to the problematic danger of wrong interpretation of intercultural communication, which may lead to various conflicts.

In relation to this, Rakšányiová (2005) talks about the shift from a culture to a phenomenon of interculturality. This basically means that the culture that has gotten through the barriers of uniqueness into the social reality shapes the communication as such. Understanding translation as one of the forms of communication leads us to the idea that translation does not exist within a strictly linguistic space but belongs to a wider and more complex space. Rakšányiová (2005) refers to it as a cultural space, which means that the transfer performed within the translation process is not only linguistic, but cultural as well.

This aspect adds the dimension of inter-/multiculturality to translation. Furthermore, similarly to Průcha, Rakšányiová emphasizes that knowing the intercultural differences is important in all areas of social life, since it may eliminate various negative associations and connotations. She also explicitly specifies that creating the text in a target language is definitely not only a linguistic issue. It is also a cultural transformation that requires a translator to take into consideration the pragmatic, semantic, and cultural context of such transfer, while paying attention to the original language and culture, and the language and culture of the target context.

Moreover, Rakšányiová opens the issue of the intercultural competence of translators by noting that a translator has to transform from a bilingual reader into an intercultural one in order to approach the whole process and be able to provide an adequate transfer.

This leads us to the question of the intercultural competence of a translator within the translation studies research. Of course, there is more than just one competence that belongs to the "required set of skills" of a professional translator. However, for the sake of our paper, it will be enough to focus on this one. In Slovak translation studies research, this competence is characterized by Gromová (2009), who states that competence lies in adopting the knowledge related to both the original and target culture in implicit and explicit confrontation, the ability of self-reflection of one's own culture in relation to the other (foreign) culture, and the ability to anticipate the cultural presuppositions, i.e. the ability to assume what information the recipient might be familiar with.

## Intercultural Identity of a Text

The identity of a text that is to be translated is determined by the difference and tension between the specifics of particular contexts and text's own specifics – artistic, expressive etc. These differences may be reflected in the un/translatability of particular culture specific references or elements. Of course, to some extent, identity of the text is influenced by the subjective approach of a translator. Together with the strategies selected during the decision-making process within translating, the translator's idiolect, interpretation, and complex understanding of a text all affect the final form in the target context. Even though these shifts performed on the expressive or semantic level may be classified according to many classifications, we do not aim to map them categorizations in this contribution.

However, it is necessary to mention that this (inter)cultural opposition is perhaps reflected most in the principles of naturalization and exoticization. These principles include strategies leading to creating covert translations, which are those with more significant naturalization tendencies, and overt translations, in which the principle of exoticization prevails (House 2015). In relation to the choice between preserving versus substituting the original identity of a text, Hochel (1990) notes that in general, we may talk about translation methods – or principles – of preserving preferring exoticization and historization, and those of substituting or implementing mostly the naturalization and modernization. Therefore, when translating, it is necessary to realize that it is precisely the set of these specific features of every text – culture, language, traditions, customs etc. – shape the identity of the text.

Vilikovský (1984) brings attention to the fact that a translator has to decide to what extent will he confront the reader with the specifics of the foreign (often unknown) context and determine which parts of its semantic and stylistic values may not be clear and understandable to the target audience. As we already mentioned, in order to embrace the cultural background, or what we call the "cultural identity" of the original more systematically, there are various classifications that help translators categorize these cultural specifics (Vilikovský, 1984; Katan, 1999; Newmark, 1995). Working with such classifications enables translators to understand the essence of particular elements of this cultural identity in order to categorize cultural references and make their further transfer easier and clearer. In this matter, we need to not only consider these concrete elements, but we need to also consider the identity they build together, because it is precisely this wider context that plays an important role in approaching the task within the complex translation process. Therefore, through the prism of translation studies research, the concept of identity is undoubtedly necessary and may be perceived from various points of view. Since we already specified (at least for now) the identity of a text, let us move to other forms of identity arising within the translation process.

## Human Identity in Translation or How Many Identities Does a Translator Need?

Before approaching the question of translator's identity, let us provide a brief comment on its "popularity" as a research focus within the field of translation studies. When emphasizing translator as a unique identity in the translation process, we might first stop for a moment and note that it is precisely a translator's identity that often stays out of the light and does not enjoy any greater attention in our translation studies history. Even though recently attention has been brought to this field of interest.

Pym (1998) notices this problem in his theoretical research on the history of translation studies. He claims that in most of the translation studies very little attention has been paid to the importance of this human aspect. A translator, who is definitely more than just one automatic part, is a stage in the process of creating a translation. As we stated before, a human who is a creative subject directly – and we believe in most cases intentionally – determines the final result of the translation process to a great extent. Moreover, Pym (1998) points out that by paying attention to the translator as a subject, the research focus may no longer be on the models and theories still influenced by typical elements of structuralism deriving from the Jacobson's understanding of the communication model.

Translators, and translations, belong to a certain social context. Social institutions (e.g. publishing houses) also belong to a certain social context. In accordance with this, Wolf and Fukari (2007) claim that social context effects all stages of a translation activity. This includes the individuals (translators) who belong to this context and the above-mentioned social institutions. We will later pay more attention to the topic of social institutions as they are one of the external factors of the translation process and determine the choice of works to be translated, production, distribution of translation, and the strategies implemented in translation.

Introducing the translation as part of a certain social context gets us further directly to the sociological dimension of translation. In Slovak translation studies, the term sociology of translation was likely first characterized by Popovič (1983), who classifies it among other subdisciplines of the so-called praxeology of translation. Importantly, Popovič emphasizes that this characteristic of translation is reflected in the genesis of translation, just as much as it is visible from the point of view of its "functioning "in general within a certain (social) context. Furthermore, Popovič adds that this sociology of translation views the translation from the perspective of social communication.

Based on the fact that Popovič perceives translation as a fact (or a phenomenon) of social and cultural awareness, he again points out to the institutions as individuals influencing the translation process through various means, such as publishing policy, cultural relations etc. Moreover, Popovič (1975) says it is the theoretical research within praxeology of translation that focuses on various factors emphasizing the sociological dimension of translation. These factors include the specific functions of literary translation criticism, the effect of cultural policy on translation program and translation business in general, the participation of editors in creating translated texts, and didactics of translation including the education of translators etc.

Popovič links this also to the question of translation criticism, which, according to him, tries to uncover or reveal the hidden identities of a work. According to Popovič, criticism's most significant ideas are based mainly on the conditions and requirements of the certain period of time. The human aspect may be seen here in the form of a subject performing the assessment while being undoubtedly influenced by these requirements, as they are closely connected to the actual value of the work within a certain context. It is necessary to emphasize the adjective "actual" in this definition, as we are convinced it is precisely this stipulation that clearly stresses the relation between translation and its reception that reflects the ever-changing and continuously developing social and cultural conditions of a certain period of time. This, we believe, to a certain extent modifies and determines the reception of such a translation.

## External Versus Internal

This leads us to the question regarding the extent to which the external and internal factors can influence the final form and value of the translation product. The external factors in our socio-political context include the presence of the so-called political gesture, education of translators etc. We consider it important to say that the external factors have influenced many fields of our cultural life or cultural space, including the translation industry. This cultural policy may have caused various factors effecting the translation situation. These factors range from minor changes made in texts during translation process to extreme situations in the form of political interventions, which led to periods of time when no translations were created due to such an intervention (Bednárová 2013). This may be perceived as one of the particular examples when one identity, especially here the identity of a target context, influences other identities, i.e. the original text, translation, translator, editor, publisher, reader etc.

Apart from these extreme forms, there are also other ways of controlling translations. These include determining the character and orientation of translation literature, which is linked to the modification or substitution of translation decisions of translators (or the whole decision-making process of creating the translations). This might include many things from the choice of texts – especially books – to be translated, including particular specific decisions and changes made on the textual level, i.e. changes in strategies, shifts etc. With regards to history for example, it is important to include that during specific periods, the choice of the translated books had to be closely and precisely examined and approved by various reviews and commissions.

There were times when there were various interventions regarding the integrity of texts in form of text manipulation and further re-writing due to censorship. There was also repressive deleting of selected parts of texts that already existed within the translation corpus. Finally, there were also interventions in the form of the disruption of continuity of translation development, which sometimes grew into the extreme forms, as afore mentioned, resulting in non-translating (Bednárová 2013).

Moreover, Bednárová comments on the various reasons for issues of unacceptable versus acceptable identity of a text. According to Bednárová (2013), the most frequent reasons included "inappropriate" topics or the specific names of "inappropriate" authors. She also states that the censorship was applied both as a preventative and repressive measure. This means that even when the translation was reviewed, marked as acceptable, and approved for publishing, it was not able to remain available on the real market. Many publications were eliminated from the market ex post and then shredded. There was also a case of indirect censorship in the form of restrictions put on imported literature. The reason might have been that the author was perceived as a possible danger for the political regime. There were also efforts to change the identity of such works to some extent in order to make them seem more acceptable in the country (especially in the twentieth century). Examples of this include auto-censorship (meta-textual camouflage) and the translation in form of adaptation (Bednárová 2013).

We agree with Bednárová (2004), who states that the translation of belles lettres and translation in general both have a significant effect on the development and character of national literatures and cultures. She also adds that this effect is mutual and that its place and its significance is undeniable. Following this approach, we are convinced that translation should be viewed as part of literature and, hence, also included in the culture of a nation. Based on this, we also understand the concept of translation as significant in terms of creating the literary and cultural space, i.e. the literary and cultural identity.

When considering the shape of translation's identity in accordance with the identity of target culture or context in general, a broader perspective emerges also in the theory of polysystems (Even-Zohar 1990). This in turn connects its existence with the social context. The literary model elaborated within this theory of polysystems is closely related to sociology, which is apparently reflected in the names of particular parts of this model. Their "new" names express their "new dimension/character/nature," i.e. their explicit social character. Compared to the Jacobson's model of communication, one can see that these new names are created on the base of perceiving them undoubtedly as parts of wider social context and social communication. These are, for instance, addresser (author) – producer, addressee (reader) – consumer, context – institution, channel – market, message – product etc.

What about the internal factors? What do we mean by this? Building on the previous facts, we consider the act of interpretation to be one of the most important, significant, and essential phases of translation process. We believe that understanding the text and understanding its identity is the first step in reaching the equivalence and preserving the invariant of the original work.

There are various different opinions on this phenomenon of interpretation. Some say that the only possible "correct" interpretation is the one
encoded by the original creator (author) of the work. To some, authors are
the ones who characterize the task of a recipient (reader) or, for the sake
of our paper, the translator. In an effort to decode the work, the translator
and reader must identify this primary or "correct" interpretation of the
work. Others, on the other hand, perceive interpretation as the sum of infinitely free interpretations that are ever-changing, continuously evolving,
developing infinitely. Therefore, according to this opinion, the interpretations and the main ideas vary from one recipient to another, from one
interpretation to another. This brings us back to the issue of identity. Does
the identity of the reader, whether they are a reader of a literary work or
the translator, matter?

Gromová (2003) characterizes the term "translation" as the final
product of various reception activities including for example reading,
understanding the text on a deeper level, getting familiar with the various
internal and external features of the text etc. Vilikovský (1984) states that
translation begins after, or even during, the first primary reception wherein
the translator gets to know the text and tries to assess it as an artistic (literary) work. A deeper or more detailed analysis enables the translator to
get familiar with the work on a deeper level, which is important especially
in order to search for the main idea or identity of a work. Among other
things, translation aims to identify the main principles of artistic figures
and observe the way the author of the original text works with the given
language. Therefore, the reader's autopsy is often enriched by the knowledge from other (secondary) sources. Based on this, it appears that this is
the phase when the translator really uses various sources and options to
get to know the object of his interest in form of uncovering its identity.

However, this concept of interpretation is very complex. According
to Vilikovský, it includes more stages or phases. Vilikovský defines these
stages as follows: the reception of the foreign (original) culture, the critical
assessment of the text, and the forming of the translation concept (like
a strategy of the work to be performed during the translation process),
which is mainly the reflection of reception of the work itself and translator's
knowledge. Therefore, we see how the blending of both cultures creates
the already mentioned inter-/multicultural identity, which is followed by

the creative phase or the reproduction of the work based on its critical reception and the translation concept.

Therefore, interpretation is understood as a sum of procedures that help uncover and reveal the semantic invariant of the original text. In this matter, Hochel (1990) adds to the issue of translation concept. He views it as a choice in the semantic value of the translation that a translator intentionally chooses, which implies the intentionality on the part of translator regarding the recipient of translation. Levý (1983) emphasizes again the social "functioning" and the social existence of a translation that is derived from the cultural requirements of a certain time (in accordance with what we referred to as an actual value of the work in the previous chapters). Furthermore, Levý adds that due to differences between language (or linguistic) systems, semantic equivalence based on strictly linguistically oriented translation transfer is not possible. In accordance with this, transferring such complex identity strictly on this linguistic level proves to be impossible. Therefore, Levý characterizes interpretation as the only option to understand the text and the only applicable way to approach the text in order to accomplish its transfer from one cultural context to another, while at the same time preserving the adequate artistic concordance between the original and the translation.

A closer examination of this issue brings us to an assumption that the interpretations may vary, not only from one individual to another (influenced by a particular personal identity) but also from one society to another – may that be understood as a society based on culture, language or any other identity while these might, of course, overlap. We believe these facts make it even more interesting to examine the matter in terms of intercultural wandering of translation.

To sum this chapter up, we would like to express our opinion that we perceive the act of interpretation as an intersection between its two actual dimensions: subjective and objective. Why do we agree with such a characteristic? The research has shown that the identity of a translated work is to a great extent determined not only by the translator's own (sometimes even personal) subjective approach. It is also determined by a wider context in form of external factors (social, cultural, political, historical etc.). As a professional, the translator shall do anything it takes to reach the highest possible adequacy and equivalence (however ambiguous and unclear these terms may be) and find the acceptable intersection between the two while preserving the communication value of a translation.

## Interpretation of Identities

Society, culture, and our own perception (and interpretation) of facts may undergo various changes in time. Some of these might be reflected in translators' decisions resulting from their subjective understanding of the information. Focusing mainly on the act of interpretation, we decided to select some of the examples from J. D. Salinger's works (and their Slovak translations) and include them here in our short demonstration of the previous theoretical background we provided.

We would like to draw attention to the act of interpretation by introducing various translations of the original works by trying to "reconstruct" the interpretations of translators that lead to particular decisions. Before we present the examples to demonstrate our statements, it is necessary to introduce the Slovak translations of these works. Translations of two short stories (the examples are from *A Perfect Day for Bananafish* and *For Esmé – With Love and Squalor*) were created by three translators Jozef Kot (later as JK, 1965), Jozef Olexa (JO, 1964) and Aňa Ostrihoňová (AO, 2015). The translations of Salinger's *The Catcher in the Rye* (1964, 1993) were both created by Viera Marušiaková. In the second case, the translation from 1993 is the edited version.

With regard to the short stories, we can see there are 50 years between the translations. Different tendencies of particular translators are visible. Moreover, one might also assume that some of the translation decisions were influenced by the accessibility of the information (or the sources to verify the information) and the technologies available at the time (the Internet etc.) Our commentaries more or less characterize the "subjective" tendencies of these translators. However, it is necessary to take into consideration the factors mentioned above. One should not "criticize" the translation without considering all the aspects determining the context it was created in.

As an example of a difference between translations that is likely caused by a lack of information or sources to verify the meanings which translators were not familiar with, we have chosen the following: *she moved the button on her Saks blouse*. A Slovak translation from 1965 for instance shows troubles understanding what a *Saks blouse* was and transfers it into Slovak as if *Saks* was a particular cut or a model of blouses. The other translation from 1964 implies it is a name of a company: *posunula si gombík na blúzke "saksového" strihu, 1965; na blúze so značkou Saksovej firmy si prešila gombičku, 1964*. The "youngest" translation – *prešila si gombík na blúzke od Saksa; 2015* – proves our previous assumption that some of the translations dating back to the sixties will be more problematic because of the lack of access to information. One may assume this reference was not known in the target context at that time and it might have been a lot more difficult to research back then as compared to present day. However, this example is still quite interesting as the translation from 1964 is correct, so in the other case it might be caused also by the translator's interpretation.

Similar changes are found in two editions of *The Catcher in the Rye* (from 1964 and 1993). A very positive finding is that almost all of the "mistakes" or inaccuracies were corrected in the later edition. For example, *the Holland Tunnel* was firstly translated as *Holandský tunel*, then corrected to *Hollandov tunel*. And of course, some changes on language level were performed in order to adapt the "identity" of the text to current conditions. In the case of these two translations, we mean especially changes caused by orthographic norms (for example *California – California – Kalifornia; Alaska – Alaska – Aljaška* etc.) or lexical adjustments (for example replacing non-standard or Czech words with Slovak (standard) ones: *desne – hrozne; kludne – pokojne; bezva – skvelý*).

Distant contexts might have caused the generalization in translations found in short stories from 1964 and 1965 when, for instance, translators likely did not expect the final recipients to be familiar with the name of a specific alcohol brand, so they decided to generalize the name and translate it as *a cocktail (mommy's going up to the hotel and have a Martini with Mrs. Hubbel; 1965: mamička si odskočí s pani Hubbelovou do hotela na koktail; 1964: mama pôjde do hotela s pani Hubbelovou na koktail)*. The translation from 2015 contains a specific name of the drink: *maminka ide do hotela a dá si s pani Hubbelovou Martini*.

A similar approach might be seen also in another example: *I remember standing at an end window of our Quonset*. This example also required a translator to anticipate the extent to which the target recipient would be familiar with this name. Three translators approached the issue differently and translated *Quonset* as *plechový barak*, *barak z vlnitého plechu* and *Nissenová vojenská búda*, in an effort to transfer the phrase to the reader in the most understandable way given the certain time period.

As mentioned before, the very nature of translation lies in transferring a text from one context to another. Therefore, it is clear and undoubtedly natural for a translator to face cultural or linguistic differences like those mentioned above. Therefore, we consider the subjective approach within interpretation to be an even more interesting issue to explore.

It might be seen in various ways and reflected for instance in preserving/ modifying expressiveness of the text, working with specific linguistic features (slang etc.), and many other forms. The following examples might also be seen as a display of translators' subjective points of view, even though we do not mean to classify such methods as solely subjective. There is no doubt in the necessity to perform shifts on expressive level of a text when translating any, especially literary, work. Such shifts are abso-lutely legitimate. However, it is quite interesting to observe the differences between the translators' choices.

The translations used in this section are again in alphabetical order: J. Kot 1965, J. Olexa 1964, A. Ostrihoňová 2015. In one of the stories, one of the protagonists describes the way her partner drove as follows: *he drove very nicely*. She wants her mother not to worry. She is not being emotional at all; she wants her mother to know she is safe with her partner. Kot translates it as *šoféroval ako boh*. The expressiveness of the text is a bit stronger than it was originally and this will have a different effect on a reader. On the other hand, Olexa and Ostrihoňová use more neutral translations and describe Seymour's driving as *šiel veľmi slušne* and *šoféroval opatrne*. Similar tendencies of Kot may be seen in another example: *I'm fine, I'm hot*. He translates it as *mám sa senzačne, skoro sa roztopím*. Compared to other two translators whose solutions are, again, more neutral (*mám sa výborne, je tu horúco; som v poriadku, je mi teplo*). Furthermore, in translation of the original: *ever since she has reached puberty*, he transfers it into Slovak as *len čo trochu vyrástla z detských sukničiek*. The other two translators, Olexa and Ostrihoňová decided to use more neutral Slovak formulations *od čias puberty* and *už od začiatku jej dospievania*.

Many other examples might be listed to prove the point that the identity of a text may be modified not only on semantic but also expressive level by changing its identity, in the sense that we change the effect it has on a recipient. We may see this also in one more example: *after Bingo he and his wife asked me if I wouldn't like to join them for a drink*. Its Slovak translations by Kot, Olexa, and Ostrihoňová respectively: *keď sme dohrali Bingo, spolu so svojou ženou ma požiadal, či by som si s nimi nešla ovlažiť pery* (JK); *po Bingu ma on i jeho žena pozvali, či by som s nimi nešla na pohárik* (JO); *po bingu ma spolu so svojou manželkou pozval na pohárik* (AO). Compared to the other translations, Kot again impresses the reader with more artistic and expressive formulations, which, we believe, will change the reader's perception of the work.

We do not mean to classify any of these approaches as right or wrong, since we do not think such a classification is possible. We only aim to point to possible shifts that can be performed and the way they may influence the works and their presentation in target culture.

However, the expressive value of the text might be not only strengthened but also lowered. It is interesting that these changes might appear not only from one translator to other. Some appear also between two editions of one translation. It might be due to a changed context or the translator's (or in some cases for instance also editor's) perspective and interpretation.

The following example does not demonstrate the weakening of the expressiveness when compared to the original, but between two translations. The original *a few pimpy-looking guys, and a few whorey-looking blondes* was translated as *pár chlapíkov, čo vyzerali ako pasáci, a pár blondín, čo vyzerali ako kurvičky* in 1964 and as *pár chlapíkov, čo vyzerali ako pasáci, a zopár blondín, čo vyzerali ako štetky* in 1993. The stronger vulgarism *kurvičky* was replaced by a softer word *štetky*.

One example of the decrease in expressiveness may be found in the analyzed short stories and their translations by Kot, Olexa, and Ostrihoňová. One of the characters tries to end a phone call with her mother by saying, *mother, this call is costing a for–*. The interpretation in the two older translations must have been a bit problematic, as both versions contain *a for–* understood as the beginning of a number (JK: *mama, tento rozhovor už stojí štyri–*; JO: *mama, tento rozhovor už bude stáť zo štyr...*). From our point of view, the author clearly did not mean to say any particular

number. However, we are convinced (or at least our own subjective interpretation leads us to the opinion) that the word was meant to be *'fortune.'*
Therefore, in Slovak it might be translated for example as *majland*. That is
probably what Ostrihoňová wanted to use in her translation *mama, tento
telefonát ťa stojí ma...* even though maybe one more letter (*maj...*) would
make the word she refers to more understandable. When discussing the
various ways, in which a translator can influence the text, these expressive
shifts are one of them.

Although we only decided to mention a few examples, we hope that
those selected demonstrate how the identity of a certain context and
the identity of a translator as a creative subject determines the identity
of the original text in its translations. Before the conclusions, we consider it important to mention also one last type of identity, even though
it was already briefly commented on in the beginning of our paper: the
identity of us, those who are trying to look at the translations through
the prism of translation criticism. When trying to assess any translation,
one becomes part of the evaluating process through commenting on the
selected methods and solutions. Consequently, every critical approach like
this might be also viewed as a form of interpretation reflecting subjective
point of view that depends on the identity, no matter how objective one
tries to be (cf. Hochel 1990).

## Conclusions

The aim of our proposed contribution was to specify the issue of identity
and its forms within the translation process. Providing also some of the
examples from J. D. Salinger's works to prove our understanding of the
issue, we tried to draw attention to some of the selected theories addressing
the question of identity within the field of translation studies.

Therefore, we have chosen the concept of identity as reflected in the
forms of a text (to be translated, focusing mainly on the literary text),
a context (as a wide term referring to the sum of various features and
conditions of a country), and the identity of the human aspect within
translation process. We do this especially with the focus on a translator
as a creative living subject and a crucial part of the process. In relation to
that, we discussed the question of interpretation as an activity reflecting

the external (objective factors), and internal (subjective perspective) world of a translator and its specifics.

Although identity has enjoyed quite a lot of "popularity" within various fields of research in the past decades, it has always been basically the main concept within translation studies research. There is a whole spectrum of creatively involved forms of identity that ultimately come together to compose a translation. However intercultural or multicultural the identity of a translation product might become during the process, the most important focus is to preserve its communication value and, especially in case of literary texts we dealt with here, enrich any other identity it meets along its intercultural journey.

# References:

BAKER, M. 2011. *In Other Words: A Coursebook of Translation.* London: Routledge, p. 332. ISBN 978-0-415-46754-4.

BASSNETT, S. 2002. *Translation Studies.* London: Routledge, p. 176. ISBN 0-415-28014-1.

BASSNETT, S. 2011. *Reflections on Translation.* Bristol: Multilingual Matters, p. 173. ISBN 978-1-84769-408-9.

BEDNÁROVÁ, K. 2013. *Dejiny umeleckého prekladu na Slovensku I: od sakrálneho k profánnemu.* [History of Literary Translation in Slovakia I: From the Sacred to the Profane.] Bratislava: Ústav svetovej literatúry SAV, p. 301. ISBN 978-80-224-1348-0.

BEDNÁROVÁ, K. 2004. *Miesto a funkcia prekladu v kultúre národa.* [Place and Function of Translation in Culture of a Nation.] In Antologie teorie uměleckého překladu. [Anthology of Theory of Literary Translation.] Ostrava: Ostravská univerzita, pp. 85–94. ISBN 80-7042-667-5.

CATFORD, J. C. 1965. *A Linguistic Theory of Translation: An Essay in Applied Linguistics.* London: Oxford University Press, p. 103. ISBN 0-19-437018-6.

*Constructing a Sociology of Translation.* 2007. Edited by Michaela Wolf and Alexandra Fukari. Amsterdam – Philadelphia: John Benjamins Publishing Company, 2007.

EVEN-ZOHAR, I. 1990. *Polysystem Studies.* In: Poetics Today, p. 1. Monotematické číslo. [Monothematic Number.]

FERENČÍK, J. 1982. *Kontexty prekladu.* [Contexts of Translation.] Bratislava: Slovenský spisovateľ, 1982.

GOUADEC, D. 2007. *Translation as a profession.* Amsterdam – Philadelphia: John Benjamins Publishing Company, p. 416. ISBN 978-90-272-1681-6.

GROMOVÁ, E. 1996. *Interpretácia v procese prekladu.* [Interpretation in the process of translation.] Nitra: Vysoká škola pedagogická, p. 136. ISBN 80-8050-076-2.

GROMOVÁ, E. 2006. *Medzikultúrny faktor v preklade a jeho reflexia v translatologickom výskume.* [Intercultural Factor in Translation and Its Reflection in Translation Studies Research.] In: Letná škola prekladu 4. Medzikultúrny a medzipriestorový faktor v preklade. [Intercultural and Interspatial Factor in Translation.] Bratislava: AnaPress, pp. 47–56. ISBN 80-89137-22-9.

GROMOVÁ, E. 2009. *Úvod do translatológie.* [Introduction to Translation Studies.] Nitra: Univerzita Konštantína Filozofa v Nitre, p. 96. ISBN 978-80-8094-627-2.

GROMOVÁ, E. – MÜGLOVÁ, D. 2005. *Kultúra – interkulturalita – translácia.* [Culture – Interculturality – Translation.] Nitra: UKF, p. 101. ISBN 80-8050-946-8.

GROMOVÁ, E. – RAKŠÁNYIOVÁ, J. 2005. *Translatologické reflexie.* [Reflections on Translation Studies.] Bratislava: Book Book, p. 74. ISBN 80-969099-2-4

HOCHEL, Braňo. 1990. *Preklad ako komunikácia.* [Translation as Communication.] Bratislava: Slovenský spisovateľ, p. 148. ISBN 80-220-0003-5.

HOUSE, J. 2009. *Translation.* Oxford: Oxford University Press, p. 122. ISBN 978-0-19-438922-8.

HOUSE, J. 2015. *Translation Quality Assessment: Past and Present.* London: Routledge, p. 160. ISBN 978-1-138-79548-8.

KATAN, R. 1999. *Translating Cultures: An Introduction for Translators, Interpreters and Mediators.* Manchester: St. Jerome Publishing, p. 271. ISBN 1-900650-14-2.

LEVÝ, J. *Umění překladu.* [Art of Translation.] Praha: Panorama, 1983.

MIKO, F. 1969. *Estetika výrazu: Teória výrazu a štýl.* [Esthetics of Expression: Theory of Expression and Style.] Bratislava: SPN, p. 292.

MIKO, F. 1978. *Tvorba a recepcia: Estetická komunikácia a metakomunikácia.* [Creation and Reception: Esthetic Communication and Metacommunication.] Bratislava: TATRAN, p. 385.

NEWMARK, P. 1999. *A Textbook of Translation.* New York: Phoenix Elt, p. 292. ISBN 0-13-912593-0.

NORD, CH. 1997. *Translating as a Purposeful Activity: Functionalist Approaches Explained.* Manchester: St. Jerome Publishing, p. 154. ISBN 1-900650-02-9.

POPOVIČ, A. 1968. *Preklad a výraz.* [Translation and Expression.] 1. vyd. Bratislava Vydavateľstvo Slovenskej akadémie vied, p. 252.

POPOVIČ, A. 1983. *Originál-Preklad.* [Original-translation.]1. vyd. Bratislava: Tatran, p. 368.

POPOVIČ, A. 1971. *Poetika umeleckého prekladu.* [Poetics of Literary Translation.] Bratislava: Tatran, p. 168.

POPOVIČ, A. 1975. *Teória umeleckého prekladu: Aspekty textu a literárnej metakomunikácie.* [Theory of Literary Translation: Aspects of Text and Literary Metacommunication.] Bratislava: Tatran, p. 293.

PRUCHA, J. 2010. *Interkulturní komunikace.* [Intercultural Communication.] Praha: Grada Publishing, p. 199. ISBN 978-80-247-3069-1.

PYM, A. 1998. *Method in Translation History.* Manchester: St. Jerome Publishing. p. 220. ISBN 1-900650-12-6.

PYM, A. 2010. *Exploring Translation Theories.* London: Routledge, p. 186. ISBN 978-0-415-55363-6.

RAKŠÁNYIOVÁ, J. 2005. *Preklad ako interkultúrna komunikácia.* [Translation as Intercultural Communication.] Bratislava: Ana Press, p. 141. ISBN 80-89137-09-1.

REISS, K. 2000. *Translation Criticism – the Potentials and Limitations: Categories and Criteria for Translation Quality Assessment.* Manchester: St. Jerome Publishing, p. 127. ISBN 1-900650-26-6.

*Routledge Encyclopedia of Translation Studies.* Edited by Mona Baker, Gabriela Saldanha. London: Routledge, p. 674. ISBN 978-0-415-36930-5.

*Translating Cultures: Perspectives on Translation and Anthropology.* Edited by Paula G. Rubel, Abraham Rosman. Oxford: Berg, p. 289. ISBN 1-85973-745-5.

TOURY, G. 1995 *Descriptive Translation Studies – and beyond.* Amsterdam – Philadelphia: John Benjamins Publishing Company, p. 311. ISBN 1-55619-687-3.

VALENTOVÁ, M. – REŽNÁ, M. 2011. *František Miko – Aspekty prekladového textu.* [František Miko – Aspects of a Translation Text.] Nitra: UKF, p. 309. ISBN 978-80-558-0010-3.

VENUTI, L. 1995. *The Translator's Invisibility: A History of Translation.* London and New York: Routledge, p. 366. ISBN 0-203-36006-0.

VILIKOVSKÝ, Ján. 1984. *Preklad ako tvorba.* [Translation as Creation.] Bratislava: Slovenský spisovateľ, p. 240.

ZAMBOR, J. 2000. *Preklad ako umenie.* [Translation asAart.] Bratislava: Univerzita Komenského, p. 239. ISBN 80-223-1407-2.

ZEHNALOVÁ, J. a kol. 2015. *Kvalita hodnocení překladu: Modely a aplikace.* [Translation Quality Assessment: Models and Application.] Olomouc: Univerzita Palackého v Olomouci, p. 343. ISBN 978-80-244-4792-6.

Lucia Valková

Department of Cultural Studies, Faculty of Arts, Constantine
the Philosopher University in Nitra

# Identity – Gender – Sex

**Abstract:** The contribution reflects on the issue of identity as a theoretical concept
in terms of gender and sex. The paper evaluates the selected theoretical concepts
and discusses the diversity of identification which has been brought about by the
current transformation and change of period discourse. Through the presentation
of examples and explorations in different gender identities, the contribution focuses
on identity as a fluid concept. The intention is to point to the multiple facets of
"identity" so as to present the different expressions as an individual project of
self-creation.

**Keywords:** Identity, gender roles, social construct, sex, self.

Identity and its theoretical constituents are problematic. For the purpose
of this paper, identity may be defined as self-definition on the basis of
self-perception. The process of self-identification is one of the first steps
of socialization. The process is followed by one's identification with the
individual's cultural surroundings, values, and the specific norms of the
society. As Slovak psychologist Viera Bačová points out, identity determination is an "open system" that is geared toward the individual's social
system. For Bačová, identity determination is an entire discourse that
varies depending on endogenous and exogenous processes. It is said that
"the ultimate is the social world, a cultural text, where defining and self-
defining takes place, and the source from which the person fully draws the
content of the defining and toward which he then points his definition."
(2003, p. 204.) In another contribution, Bačová follows the ideas of Rom
Harré[1] and Jill Johnstone, who, while defining the notion of identity, state
that "identities of people are not willingly and freely created products of

---

1   "People are what they are convinced to be – and their conviction about what
    they are, is actually what they were told to be by the greatest authorities."

introspection or unproblematic reflection of the private sanctuary of the 'inner self.' On the contrary, they are exceedingly 'conceived' from certain ideological frameworks that have created a dominant social order or system for their preservation." (2001, p. 123). Thus, identity necessarily moves from the essentially individual matter to the political sphere. The creation of identity is founded upon the basis of what the society accepts and deems legitimize and what the society opposes and marginalizes. Identity is not only a mean of self-realization of individuality and uniqueness. Identity is also the product of certain elements of the social system that circumscribes the individual's possibilities.

In the sense of primary socialization, identity appears primarily to be a type of stabilizing element, since in the next stages of personality development, the individual offers the space for our own realization.

Both endogenous and exogenous aspects effect the process of self-identity creation, which as a result has an influence on the process of perception and personality formation. The onset of postmodernism, automation and regrouping of the real and the virtual world only support multiplicity, fluidity, fragmentation in society, which are also directly reflected in the survival of the individual and in creation of the self. This condition was also mentioned by the Polish sociologist Zygmunt Bauman, who states: "Identity ... is something that is being constructed and that can (at least in principle) be constructed in various ways." (2006, p. 27)

The ongoing processes of globalization accelerates transcultural transitions and opens up a wide range of possibilities for man to identify himself. These developments present multiplicity of values, traditions, cultures, and ways of life that can be reflected in self-projection and identity formation. This is how the Slovak cultural studies specialist, Kristína Jakubovská, sees the issue. She holds the outlook that because we multiply identities by widening the reference groups and the list of values we refer to while identifying "the exclusive biological determinism and the resulting primary stability of identity are no longer valid ... the more topical is actually its contextuality following the constructivist discourse." (Jakubovská, 2016, p. 216) Sociologists Peter L. Bergmen and Thomas Luckmann emphasize man as a being shaped in relation to the natural and human environment. "From the moment of birth, the development of the human organism, as well as the development of a greater part of its biological essence as such, is subjected to a constant socially determined influence." (1999, p. 52) The constraints that society creates are conditioned, in particular, by the cultural framework and social structures in which it operates. However, on the other hand we do not only create our own identity, but adapt ourselves to everyday situations, in which we highlight a certain aspect of our identity. By functioning in a certain socio-cultural reality, we are forced to take on a role and create mutual connections, but the way of a self- identity formation gives us a certain level of freedom. Therefore, identity presents a certain specificity that we do not only create but also communicate externally. We express our certain authenticity, integrity, otherness and, at the same time, connection with other members of society.

The Slovak theoretician Erich Mistrík holds the identity of the individual as made of "ductile" material. Mistrík states that identity is both created by every interaction with the surrounding world and at the same time requires self-awareness of the subject-creator of the change and the object of the change.

> My identity, my otherness arises and forms only in relation to the other. ... The culture and otherness of the other person is therefore not something that is outside of me and independent of me. By my relationship to him I form his vision of the world and his identity – as well as he forms my vision of the world and my identity. His culture and his otherness are becoming the part of my personal culture. Our personal cultures are either two mirrors that reflect each other, or two liquids of different densities that pour together, mix, and separate from each other. ... My personal identity and my personal culture are therefore varied and moving, it is the intersection of many relationships ... In those other mirrors I find myself. It is my self-reflection, that is constantly changing, as my relationships with other identities and other self-reflections change. ... It is something like the deconstruction of my cultural and personal identity (Mistrík, 2009, pp. 68–69).

There are two important processes in the creation of identity: the process of self-reflection, self-formation, and the influence the society has on self-image. Even though the present time is referred to as a "symbolic supermarket of identities," some psychological directions underestimate man's abilities in the self-formation processes. Czech psychologist and theoretician, Ivo Čermák, denies the implicit assumption of various psychological metaphors (behaviorism, neuropsychology, etc.), stating that "man has no capacity to become aware, to respond to the challenges and pressures of social structures, to be creative and to develop new ways of life" (Čermák, 2001, p. 82). The above-mentioned metamorphoses and regrouping of characteristics within the framework of gender affiliation or the queer concept are a clear example that man's creativity in the self-creation and survival is multifaceted. This aspect may also be interpreted in a more negative light. The above-mentioned psychological direction of behaviorism, which is also represented by Sandra Bem with her theory of "self-attribution" (self-assessment based on characteristics), points to the intrasubjective activity of an individual. According to American sociologist Viktor Gecas, "self" usually refers to the process of reflection that emanates from the dialectic between "myself" and "me." The product of this reflection is "self-concept" – "individual concept of self as a psychic, social, spiritual or moral being" (Gecas, 1982, pp. 1–3).

According to Černák: "self (without which there can be no identity) is rather such a concept of human being, in which any creation of the meaning is socially constructed and can be understood as a derivative of a subset of social, cultural and historical conditions (social constructivism) and the presence of a self-creation resource" (2009, pp. 82–83). Self represents some kind of subjective improvisation and adaptation to the social reality during the process of self-creation. An important element in this is the ability to self-reflect and engage in self-assessment based on one's relation to a socio-cultural reality and one's place within this reality. As Jakubovská states, the identity as a stabilizing element of a socio-cultural position involves fragmentation. There is an internal fragmentation due to the amount of identification connections and roles that shape us. Moreover, these connections are often contradictory, which only adds to the fragmentation (Jakubovská, 2016, p. 116.) These contradictions and fragmentation stem from the diversity of codes and symbolic system that operates in the cultural community. The importance of language in verbalizing self-identity is justified. As Czech sociologist Martin Fafejta says, "if a certain identity is impossible, it is not because people of this identity do not exist, but because we do not understand it as an identity, and we do not have resources for its creation- language " (2004, p. 45).

The concept of identity, especially in the humanities, has developed into a wide definition with significant ambiguity, evidenced by the gradual blurring of the core concept. Moreover, this was a result of this conceptual intangibility, the plurality of postmodern and poststructuralist theories, multiculturalism, the "identity crisis" that the German American developmental psychologist and psychoanalyst Erik Erikson described in the 1960s.

The notion of identity may be seen from several aspects. The most interesting being the concept of identity in the social sciences, which was presented first by sociologist Rogers Brubaker and historian Frederic Cooper. They identified five of the most important meanings and ways of perceiving identity in the social sciences:

1. Identity as an opposition to interest, an effort to conceptualize noninstrumental modes of social and political action.[2]
2. Identity as a collective phenomenon, which denotes the sameness among members of a certain group or category.[3]
3. Identity as a core aspect of "selfhood" (individual or collective) or as a fundamental condition of social being.[4]

---

2 Emphasis on the manner in which action-individual or collective-may be governed by particularistic self-understanding rather than by putatively universal self-interest. It involves three related but distinct constraints in ways of conceptualizing and explaining action: 1. Self-understanding and self-interest, 2. Particularity and universality, and 3. Ways of construing social location. Social location means something different in the two cases: for identity theorizing, it means position in a multidimensional space defined by particularistic categorical attributes (race, ethnicity, gender, sexual orientation). For instrumentalist theorizing, it means position in a universally conceived social structure (position in the market, the occupational structure, etc.)

3 It may be understood objectively (as a sameness "in itself") or subjectively (as an experienced, felt, or perceived sameness). The sameness is expected to manifest itself in solidarity, in shared dispositions or consciousness, or in collective action. This usage is found especially in the literature on social movements, on gender, and on race, ethnicity, and nationalism.

4 Identity is invoked to point to something allegedly deep, basic, abiding, or foundational. This is distinguished from more superficial, accidental, fleeting, or contingent aspects or attributes of the self, and is understood as something to be valued, cultivated, supported, recognised, and preserved. This usage is characteristic of a certain strand of the psychological literature, especially as influenced by Erikson, though it also appears in the literature on race, ethnicity, and nationalism.

4. Identity as a product of social or political action.[5]
5. Identity as fluctuating and fragmented nature of the contemporary "self"[6] (2000, pp. 6–8).

Bačová points to the perception of the identity concept from a socio-cultural and political perspective. Our vision of the world affects the way we live and live a certain kind of life. In social constructivism context, identity focuses not "accuracy" or "objectivity" but rather on social and political functions. The new theoretical frameworks of psychology explore the notion of identity "in socio-cultural and political contexts – mutual connections among people, which "add" the identity to these people, i.e. offer for acquisition" (2001, p. 124). That is why the sociocultural aspect of identity is more important than traditional psychology. The term "identity" can be also defined as the self-defining of the person, which express how a person can be distinguished (authentic) from other people in his or her environment and for other people. It is in this way that his social status and role in his or her community becomes legitimate. The meaning and significance of person's activity is determined by their relation to others and the community as a whole, including the significance of the person's life story as ascribed by the person and by others (2003, pp. 203–204).

The race and gender to which one belongs is another important aspect of the individual's identity and plays a role in determining the individual's identity in various ways. Race and gender have become an instrument and object of theoretical and political origins of feminist movements and post-feminist tendencies. American post-structuralist philosopher, Judith Butler, who deals with the field of feminist and gender theories, pointed to race and gender as representing the mimetic aspect of identity. As Butlers

---

5   Identity is invoked to highlight the processual, interactive development of the kind of collective self-understanding, solidarity, or groupness "that can make collective action possible. In this usage, found in certain strands of the" new social movement "literature," "identity" is understood both as a contingent product of social or political action and as a ground or basis of further action.
6   Identity is invoked to highlight the unstable, multiple, fluctuating, and fragmented nature of the contemporary "self." This usage is found especially in the literature influenced by Foucault, post-structuralism, and post-modernism.

states, race and gender are "a type of constantly imitating formation that is perceived as a reality" (2003, p. 8).

## The Nature of Sex

Sex is a biological characteristic which defines the physiological differences between individuals based on anatomy of the human body and chromosomal differences. On the basis of biologically, conditioned diversity or the duality of men and women is preserved. Moreover, this duality is also reflected in the division of social life.

Sexual identity is based on biological determinants and represents the innate part of personal identity. The development of the biological sex takes place during the second trimester of pregnancy. Sexual identity is a subjectively perceived part of self-image which includes one's primary and secondary sexual characteristics and social roles attributed to a given sex. Based on the awareness of one's own body and sex, sexual identity represents the innate part of the identity and arises from biological determinants. It is a mental sex that determines whether a person feels like a man or a woman regardless of his or her biological sex. During lifetime, a person creates an ensemble of emotional and cognitive experiences that influence thinking and feeling, including interests and professions (Fifková 2008, pp. 13–14).

Furthermore, socio-cultural factors influence our life experiences. Socio-cultural factors determine social respect and attribution of male and female activities and characteristics. A set of characteristics, which are traditionally attributed to a given sex, create cultural stereotypes. Dominance, assertiveness, spatial imagination, and decisiveness are often attributed to men, while women are more commonly submissive, emotional, empathetic, communicative. The external manifestations of sexual identity in society are the sex roles we acquire through upbringing, especially during initial socialization. Upbringing is something that helps us be the part of the world, where the gender division is preserved.

Human anatomy, the division into men and women on the basis of sexual organs, was an impetus for a further research. The influence and tendencies of constructivism, the activity of feminist movements, and the onset of postmodernist tendencies opened up a new door for polemics to reevaluate the socially constructed patterns of behavior and self-presentation. There is a possibility to observe the stabilizing element of the social system exactly in the constructed ways of behavior, which have been preserved as formulas, which are habitual[7] since "habit creates a stable background" (Berger, Luckmann, 1999, p. 57). Each role that has become a model performs as a skeleton for institutionalization based on predictable and expected standardized activities and behavior of individuals. This standardized type of procedure may change with interaction. The reality created in this process varies. The turning point is during the educational process when social reality and its system are transferred to the next generation and the constructed reality is objectivized. It becomes the only possible world and learned activities, behavior, actions in different situations are considered natural.

American sociologists Claire M. Renzetti and Daniel J. Curran emphasize that "human sex [is] a biological characteristic (being a man or a woman) [and] serves as a basis for the construction of a social category called gender (masculinity or femininity)" (Renzetti, Curran, p. 20) The biological determinism to be male or female is natural only in a certain culture. However, in Slovakia and the Czech Republic, emphasis is placed on the fact that the newborn who was born as an intersex[8] fits one of two sexes. The natural reaction of doctors and parents is the sex reassignment surgery based on tests. On the other hand, In India, the third gender is considered to be a gift and a tremendous honor for the individual. Not only does such an individual receive great esteem in society but is also believed to possess supernatural powers. Even human nature is, in this case, culturally and socially constructed. Why is naturalness considered to be unnatural at some point and has to be changed? Can individuals who do not fit the category threaten the system? When considering societies that are based on a two-sex model, there are available resources, which are used to maintain the balance of this model. One of the reasons is also the effort not to threaten the reproduction process. This indicates

---

7   The notion is taken from BERGER, P. L., LUCKMANN, T., 1999, p. 56
8   Although rarely, occurs the form of the third sex, hermaphrodite, intersex. It is an individual that is born with both male and female sexual features, or these sexual organs are not clearly identifiable.

that body and physicality become independent entities subjected to discourse practices. In this respect M. Fafejta adds: "biological differences are highlighted by socialization; sex differences are strengthened by gender differences" (2004, p. 36).

## "Unwritten Rules"

The distinction and division between biological sex and gender, as a culturally related category, has significantly influenced the direction not only of feminist efforts but also the understanding of the social sphere of life and its exploration. Gender, its significance, and impact on social structures have extended to two opposing theories: biological essentialism and social constructivism. The first approach to gender, biological essentialism, holds that gender is determined by the human anatomy together with innate sexual characteristics. The second approach, social constructivism, is based on the assumption that gender is a strictly social category and is therefore constructed and transformed by the influence of social, cultural, and economic interaction. All aspects associated with the existence of a person in the society are the result of the construction of reality, which is often difficult to distinguish from naturalness.

The distinction between sex and nature, and gender and culture, have a meeting point in the symbolic connections between woman – nature, and man – culture. However, a person needs cornerstones to interact with the rest of the world, allowing him to understand and predict situations. One of the cornerstones, according to Iris M. Young, is gender. Young, ahead of her time, made the claim three decades ago that "the concept of a gender can be considered as the basic organizational principle of understanding the culture" (Young, 1984, In: Heller, 2005, p. 5). Nevertheless, as Czech psychologist Daniel Heller later adds: "the forming of male and female beings cannot be understood primarily as a psychological process or a social role, but as a universal principle of social and cultural life, which is manifested in individual psyche, metaphysics and ideologies of society" (2005, p. 5).

In the context of a socially constructed reality that also includes the sex-change of intersex or the external gender presentation of men and women, there is an interesting concept of "biopower," which was first introduced by French philosopher Michel Foucault. Foucault first devoted himself to the study of the microcosm of power exercitation when the state implemented discursive practices through three domains of human subjectivity: the body, the individual, and the population. One of the areas where discursive practices of power control have been implemented through the centuries is the sexuality of a man and his body. Through the construction of sexuality, gender, and sex, society gains the power over an individual and determines his place in the society. It creates a normative framework, a contemporary discourse grasped institutionally on several levels at the same time. The goal of such a power restriction of sexuality was to organize individual development, both physical and mental. "Between the state and individual, sex became an issue and a public issue no less" (Foucault, 1999, p. 34). Another power grasp of sexuality was the condemnation and especially the discursive grasp of various perversions in the form of "nervous disorders" (Foucault, 1999, p. 38), where, for example, even avoiding procreation. Defining the institution of marriage, acceptability of sexual intercourse only in marriage, the validity of which is contingent upon church marriages.

These mechanisms have operated through the centuries in order to restrict the will and identity of a person and preserve the sovereignty of the state over the individual. The body became a means through which the power of the state was able to grow. In the context of determining one's own individuality based on social norms, Foucault speaks of the state creating "biopower" over individuals, their bodies and identities. The body has become the subject of control. Multiplicity in individuality was determined by the limits provided by the state. Body, which we could perceive as neutral, acquires political significance in the society (Foucault, 1999, pp. 23–50).

Despite the various institutional mechanisms and power structures, biopower implementation is declining and fading as the spectrum of the three domains of human subjectivity expands. The three domains are: the body, the individual and the population, which society constructs. Due to factors such as globalization, automation, postmodern tendencies, and deconstruction theories, etc., the boundaries of male and female identity, stereotypes about gender behavior, and the inclusion of these social norms are fading. Moreover, these aspects cause the "identity problem," which occurs when identity may be always different and as a result evokes the feeling of an unstable existence. In such an instance, identity becomes an unavoidable mission. The necessity of choice and free formation of identity has become the destiny of a modern man. Indeed, the anonymity of the crowd provides a shelter, but at the same time, it complicates self-seeking and the legitimate pursuit of one's own place in a society that could be respected by the surrounding world. As Bauman pointed out, "while in traditional society the identity of individuals is being involved in a stable system of social status and roles within small closed communities, the mass conditions and anonymous society indicate the identity issue as an urgent individual challenge" (2006, p. 25). On the other hand, "the uncertainty and ambiguity of the communicating elements are not a manifestation of the defect of the system but a condition of its vitality" (Bauman, 2006, p. 20).

## "Symbolic Supermarket of Identities"

The modern phenomenon is the queer concept, which points to the breadth of sex-gender-sexual otherness. As M. Fafejta notes, today the concept of the modern period may be explained as a "symbolic supermarket of identities" (2016, p. 192) that provides almost unlimited choices. On the one hand, the society puts pressure on people and determines the acceptability and normality of identity. On the other hand, "the consumer's desire to alternate new and new is extending, which is connected with the inability to accept something definitively and to be satisfied with that" (Fafejta, 2016, p. 192).

The queer concept hides in itself a great plurality of meanings from its very origin. It is based on definite ambiguity and elasticity. Sociologist Steven Epstein says that "queer" opposes the convention of social norms in connection with sexuality, so as to eliminate pre-stereotyped labelling. The queer category includes anyone who deviates from defined boundaries or categories, and wants to live differently, regardless of their sexual orientation, gender presentation, or sex (Epstein, In: Fafejta, 2016, p. 193). Fafejta adds: "The queer concept is a political category, because it wants to change power discourses that understand identity as something fixed and unchanging, what the individual is born with and must obey" (Fafejta,

2016, pp. 193–194). According to the New Zealand theorist Annamarie Jagos, this concept includes and at the same time covers a certain cultural marginalized sex-gender-sexual self-identification and the process of forming a theoretical model. Originally, the model was meant to develop studies of traditional homosexual orientation.

Despite model's ambition, it is not entirely considered to be an academic category (Jagose, 1996, p. 72). As British theorist Katherine Watson states, the queer concept based on critical theories and actions used poststructuralist deconstruction techniques to uncover the historical confirmation of sexual subjects. Moreover, Watson notes that in this process we may observe the fragility of the so-called stable identities of heterosexuality and homosexuality that depend on the successful gender presentation (Watson, 2005, pp. 67–68). Watson understands "queer theory, as one among many of the useful ways of understanding the myriad complexities of identity, oppression and group dynamics" (Watson, 2005, p. 68). As trans activist Leslie Feinberg says, "all our communities break down all boundaries of the sex and sexuality and related to them restrictions. And the junction point between these communities is the struggle for the right to freely express the individual's personality" (Feinberg, 2000, p. 8)" Despite the increasing openness of the presentation, there are still few people who use the queer concept. They do not take the risk in highlighting their otherness in order to distinguish themselves. Often, in common interaction, one's own identity is hidden. According to M. Fafejtu being queer is not necessarily about crossing borders and mixing behavior patterns. It is more about realizing one's own identity as something more than a personal characteristic, or even a hobby. It is common for a person to be in contact with the queer community, rather than focus on its existence (2016, pp. 200–201).

The queer concept is one of the examples of the disintegration of traditional social structures highlighted by Bauman. Social forms of acceptable behavior, institutions that seek to control personal freedom can no longer fulfil their functions and maintain their existence. They disintegrate and dissolve faster than they are established. The forms of behavior that are being created or already exist do not have enough time to establish and create a reference framework for human behavior and actions. They do not become an integral and fixed part of "life projects" of individuals.

They lose their meaning and help to create the "flow" of time with deceptively endless possibilities of self-realization and self-identification, which may make a men drown (Bauman, 2008, pp. 9, 16–17).

## Conclusions

Identity as a term has lost stabilizing character. Especially in the humanities, as the American sociologist Rogers Brubaker and historian Frederic Cooper have pointed out, there is a great deal of ambiguity and hence some emptiness of its meaning. As we tried to point out in the current paper, fragmentation, plurality, and infiniteness are also reflected in the self-creation of individuals. We could consider this as an aspect of the time period or due to the influence of multiculturalism where national identity is also lost in people. Man, travels and is thus more oriented toward wider viewpoints, losing contact with family and home. The felt sense of the loss of cornerstones during the process of self-reflection is deepening. During the gradual formation of our personalities we are confronted with countless influences, from mass media and literature, to travelling. That is why it is possible to observe transcultural overlaps, even though we will never cross the borders of the home state.

Despite identity being unique to each of us, there is a clear understanding and coexistence within the society. Therefore, neither the queer concept nor its multiplicity should automatically be a negative factor. We cannot create something in society that could not exist in it in anyway. We would not have the means of expression to reflect the absolute difference, and without them we would not be able to identify such otherness. As mentioned in the paper, the identity of an individual is fragmented. Individuals may identify themselves with anything, even if it leads to a conflict. Bauman points to the blurring of boundaries writing that "the truly postmodern personality is characterized by the absence of identity" (Bauman, 2006, p. 35). R. Brubacker and F. Cooper agree with poststructuralist and postmodernist ideas of M. Foucault saying that in the context of current period of time, the identity is fluid and volatile. Yet identity remains a process of lifelong self-formation, a value in itself for each of us. The consciousness of integrity and a specific form of adaptation to transformation in society, allows us to be an authentic part of society.

# References:

BAČOVÁ, Viera: Osobná identita – konštrukcie – text – hľadanie významu. IN: ČERMÁK, I. HŘEBÍČKOVÁ M., MACEK, P. (ed): Agrese, identita, osobnost. Brno: Psychologický ústav AV ČR, Sdružaní SCAN, Tišnov, 2003, pp. 241–248. ISBN 80-86620-06-9.

BAČOVÁ, Viera: Problém identity v sociálnej psychológii. IN: BIANCHI, G. (Ed.): Identita, zdravie a nová paradigma. Human Communication Studies, Vol. 7. Veda, Bratislava, 2001. pp. 121–125. ISBN 80-224-0702-X.

BAUMAN, Zigmund: Tekuté časy. Život ve věku nejistoty První vydání. Praha: Academia, 2008, p. 109. ISBN 978-80-200-1656-0.

BAUMAN, Zigmund: Úvahy o postmoderní době. První vydání. Praha: Slon, 2006, p. 165. ISBN 80-86429-11-3.

BERGER, Peter L. – LUCKMANN, Thomas: Sociální konstrukce reality: Pojednání o sociologii vědění. Brno: Centrum pro studium demokracie a kultury, p. 214. ISBN 80-85959-46-1.

BRUBAKER, Rogers, COOPER, Frederick: Beyond Identity. IN: Theory and Society. [online] Kluwer Academic Publishers, California. 2000, pp. 1–47 [cit. 2019-01-15]. Retrieved from: <http://www.sscnet.ucla.edu/soc/faculty/brubaker/Publications/18_Beyond_Identity.pdf>.

ČERMÁK, Ivo: Príběhy žité a vyprávěné. IN: BIANCHI, Gabriel: Identita, zdravie a nová paradigma. Bratislava: SAV VEDA, 2001, p. 192. ISBN: 80-224-0702-X.

FAFEJTA, Martin: Sexualita a sexuální identita. Sociální povaha přirozenosti. Praha: Portál, 2016, p. 240. ISBN 978-80-262-1030-6.

FAFEJTA, Martin: Úvod do sociologie pohlaví a sexuality. Prvé vydanie. Věrovany: Nakladatelství Jan Piszkiewicz ve Věrovanech, 2004, p. 159. ISBN 80-86768-06-6.

FEINBERG, Leslie: Pohlavní štvanci. První vydání. Praha: G plus G, s.r.o., 2000, p. 173. ISBN 80-86103-32-3.

FIFKOVÁ, Hana. a kol.: Transsexualita a jiné poruchy pohlavní identity. 2. vydání. Praha: Grada Publishing, a.s., 2008, p. 216. ISNB 978-80-247-1696-1.

FOUCAULT, Michel: Dějiny sexuality I. Praha: Herrmann a synové, 1999, p. 189.

GÁL, E. – MARCELLI, M. (ed.): Za zrkadlom moderny. 1. zborník o filozofickom postmodernizme na Slovensku. Bratislava: Archa, 1991, p. 320. ISBN 80-7115-025-8.

GECAS, Viktor, 1982. The Self-concept. IN: *Annual Review of Sociology*. [online] Vol. 8 (1982), pp. 1–33. [cit. 2018-12-15] Retrieved from: <https://campus.fsu.edu/bbcswebdav/institution/academic/social_sciences/sociology/Reading%20Lists/Social%20Psych%20Prelim%20Readings/III.%20Self%20and%20Identity/1982%20Gecas%20-%20The%20Self-Concept.pdf>.

HELLER, D. Maskulinita a feminita v dějinách psychologie. IN: *Psychologické dni 2004: Svět žen a svět mužů. Polarita a vzájemné obohacování: sborník příspěvků z konference Psychologické dny, Olomouc 2004.* [online] Olomouc, 2005. [cit. 2018–12–02] Retrieved from: <http://cmps.ecn.cz/pd/2004/texty/pdf/heller.pdf>.

JAGOSE, A.. *Queer Theory. An Introduction.* New York: NYU Press, 1996, p. 156. ISBN-13: 978-0814742341

JAKUBOVSKÁ, Kristína: Od multikultúrnosti a internacionalizácie k revitalizácii tradícií. František Šalé – nakladatelství Albert, 2017. P. 156. ISBN 978-80-7326-275-4.

MACEK, Petr: Kdo má nárok na identitu? Může (vývojová) psychologie inspirovat sociální vědy? [online] 2009. [cit. 2018-12-03] Retrieved from: http://ispo.fss.muni.cz/uploads/2download/pol_mob_identita.pdf.

MISTRÍK, Erich: Multikultúrna výchova a kultúrna identita. In: GAŽOVÁ, V. Úvod do kulturológie. Bratislava: Katedra kulturológie, FF UK, 2009, p. 107. ISBN 80-7121-315-2.

WATSON, Katherine: Queer Theory. IN: Group Analysis. [online]. 2005. Sage Journals online, 38; pp. 67–81. [cit. 2018—01]. Retrieved from: <http://gaq.sagepub.com/cgi/content/refs/38/1/67>.

MA Lucia Valková

Department of Cultural Studies

l.valkova88@gmail.com

This paper is published under the call UGA 2017 Personal ID No I-17–209–02.

Michal Kočiš

Department of Cultural Studies, Faculty of Arts, Consantine
the Philosopher University in Nitra

# Independent Cultural Centers as the Place for Creating Identity

**Abstract:** The presented text deals with Slovak independent cultural centers and circumstances that led to the establishment of the first independent cultural centers. Through selected points, it tries to point out to the character of development from community and civic initiatives to established cultural centers. The main goal of the presented text is to point out to the broader context in which we may perceive these centers as places where people find, build, and shape their identity.

**Keywords:** Independent, cultural centers, identity, community.

> *Since the era of Greek philosophers, the majority
> of thinkers have considered it natural that there
> exists something like human nature, something that
> is the essence and uniqueness of man. There were
> several opinions on what creates this uniqueness,
> however, the thinkers agreed on the fact that there
> exists something that makes man a man. Human
> was defined as a being gifted by brain, as a social
> being able to create tools (*homo faber*) or as a being
> creating symbols.*
>
> – E. Fromm

Independent cultural centers or even other venues and places of independent culture and art could be perceived as places where individuals find,
build, and form their identity. Today, these centers are considered cultural institutions, not established by the state. We also encounter various
arguments about its dependence or independence, which is closely related
to the identity of the individual centers. To understand the issue, it is essential to know the history. At the same time, if we want to understand what

preceded center's establishment and where we can find the roots of their identity, we need to become familiar with terms like *independence, alternative,* and *metanoia.*

Ondřej Daniel (2017) refers to Yurchak who on examples of various art groups shows how in the era of late socialism, the alternative was born, which by its approaches and values forgets about what is, looking back, often called political resistance. Daniel continues: "According to Yurchak, in this sense, subcultural phenomena resign on political expression and try to live a life different from the one lived by ordinary citizens, in boiler rooms on building sites or the outskirts of towns, and they create their distinctive language and the way of expression (be that artistic or just provocative) that often shocks the society." This may be understood in a way that the need to be independent arises from a natural need to live differently, to search for something that makes us free and to look for the essence of our own nature or identity. An inevitable part is the inner engagement in an individual, proceeding to a collective. By individual actions and by interest, alternative societies and communities emerge, which spontaneously leads to production of DIY.[1]

If we move back to the beginning of the 1990s and think about the intentions within the cultural frame of Slovakia, we may say that it was the alternative and independent communities that were engaged in the public space with the aim to bring something that was missing. Slávo Krekovič (2016), the co-author of the book *BA!! Miesta živej kultúry (1989–2016),* explains that "a living breeding ground of the uncertain durability interwoven by music clubs, galleries, artistic and social knots of various kinds created by citizens, emerged with the enthusiasm and urge to bring something that was missing: a piece of creative energy, of human and poetic nature, and of the generation's spirit; moreover, of a sudden but important feeling of possession. Who else should the city belong to, if not to the people who live here and create?" The activities of the people who are

---

1  DIY – "Do It Yourself," works on a principle according to which a person, without any professional help, creates a useful thing which serves him and others, instead of buying it in a corporate company and so supporting it. This principle is used by many subcultures. The DIY phenomenon represents an alternative to the majority culture.

active citizens and think as a community preceded the establishment of the first independent cultural centers and were directly related to the political situation and to the cultural vacuum of the nineties. Based on individual historical events, it may be said that the critical eras give greater opportunity to artistic and cultural development than the eras of consolidation and security.

## History of Independent Cultural Centers

The beginnings of independent cultural centers in Slovakia date back to post-revolution years, when civil activists began to form various initiatives and communities that aimed to bring in independent culture and art. Soon after November 1989, the initiatives were mainly without any stable aim e.g. music clubs, independent galleries, and cultural-artistic communities. It has to be said that in its beginnings, many of the initiatives ended very quickly. This cycle, so to speak, had its reasons. For instance, there was frequent fluctuation, inappropriate cultural policy, and unstable setting. In the late 90's, the situation slowly began to change. There was more activity, especially in large cities, which to some extent had to do with the change of the political establishment. The first initiatives were formed thanks to these activities at the beginning of the new millennium. Today, these initiatives are known as independent cultural centers because of their continuous professional work. Žilina, Bratislava, and Košice may also be counted among those responsible for development of independent culture in Slovakia after 1989. Stanica Žilina-Záriečie,[2] in Bratislave A4 – priestor súčasnej kultúry (space of contemporary culture),[3] and in Košice the civil association Bona Fide initiated the project Inter City Culture Train, which was the first independent cultural center in Eastern Slovakia, were based on these first contemporary centers. It is important to emphasize that the members of the civil association Bona Fide in Košice initiated various projects of revitalization and cultivation of public venues since its creation. This was the case until a project in which they cooperated with the Košice County in order to reconstruct a former industrial object and so

---

2  www.stanica.sk.
3  www.a4.sk.

open the Tabačka Kulturfabrik,[4] the biggest independent cultural center in Slovakia. It should be said that in Slovakia other various activities have had roots in activities of civil associations since 1989.

Picture 1

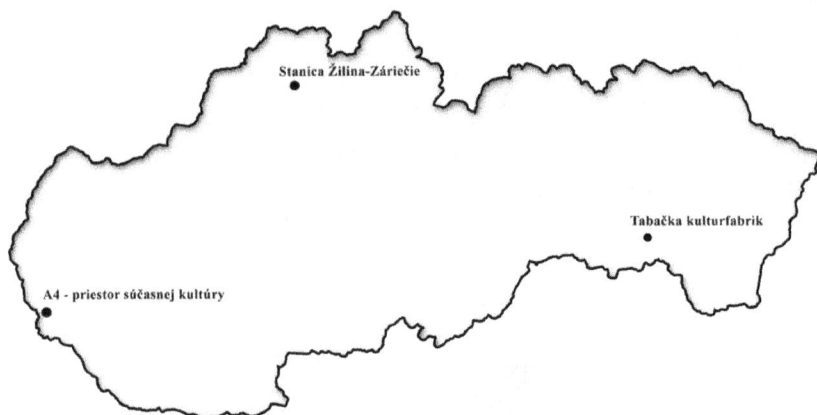

The abovementioned cities determine three main geographical points of the country. At the same time, they determine the important bases for the further development of independent cultural centers in Slovakia. The activities of various independent initiatives and communities in other Slovak cities formed new independent cultural centers based on the example of the existing independent cultural centers. The first initiatives began in larger cities, then continued in smaller cities, which became equally important during the years. These initiatives include Záhrada – centrum nezávislej kultúry in Banská Bystrica (a center of independent culture),[5] Divadlo Pôtoň,[6] also known as Centrum umenia a kreativity Bátovce (a center of art and creativity), which crosses the regions's borders with its initiatives. From 2000 to 2010, the developing cultural centers worked on gaining a suitable venue and materials. Once Slovakia became the member of the European Union, these centers received financial grants to

---

4   www.tabacka.sk.
5   www.zahradacnk.sk.
6   www.poton.sk.

develop their programs. It was then that they could also start using various European mobilities for artists, a development which brought new forms of art and creative methods to Slovak cultural space. Miroslav Ballay writes: "It is more than obvious that independent cultural and artistic centers integrated and brought together local artists and foreign partners in an inspiring way and hence provided international artistic cooperation" (2017). In his study "Dramaturgické línie nezávislých kultúrnych centier Stanica Žilina-Zariečie a Záhrada – centrum nezávislej kultúry," Ballay speaks of educational potential of independent cultural centers: "Often, it was the independent cultural and artistic centers that provided people with current topics, connected them with the places of cultural centers and with their cultural heritage" (2017). It was this part of Ballay's research activities that helped us name the activities and parts creating the identity of an independent cultural center. This way, we can see the development and support for communities in the place where an independent cultural center operates and fosters education, revitalization, and cultivation of public venues. After 2010, stabilization began. Stable centers have their own structures, drama, and plans for further development. Independent cultural centers became an inherent part of cultural and public world. In some cases, they even replace the missing or poorly functioning cultural organizations governed by the state.

## Identity of Independent Cultural Centers Versus Economic Dependency

Above, we aimed to explain how the identity of an individual, of a member of various subcultures and communities, influences the development of identity of venues now known as independent cultural centers. By presenting a brief history of important centers of independent culture, we illustrated the core of identity of independent cultural centers. It is understandable that the first independent cultural centers during their over 15-year-long history have changed their appearance. However, what is important is what is inside: their inner identity. Nowadays, their independence is questioned. Usually, "independence" is understood as that which is not run by the state. This means that the state cannot in any way intervene with its integrity.

The term "independence" is becoming associated with media and funding. In the case of media, we talk about the so-called alternative and independent media. Taking the current political situation into consideration, terms "independence" and "alternative" have negative connotations. By this, we seek to point out how these terms have been changing their meaning and connotations in society since late socialism and up to today's post-factual era. We also point out what Boris Ondreička (2017), Slovak artist, singer and curator, says. He states that the term "alternative," which we understood as the synonym of the term "independence," is reactive. Meanwhile, we watch how the phrase "alternative" reaches the mainstream. Along the same lines, Michal Kaščák (Fuják 2006) says that the term "alternative" has become overused and people tend not to use it.

Our previous research confirms the relevancy of his statement, and at this point we would add that the use of the terms "alternative" and "independence" is not only avoided by those who attend the centers of independent culture but also some of the centers themselves. They rather call themselves cultural and artistic centers or cultural-community centers. This does not necessarily have to do with blurring the borders and "alternative" getting into the mainstream. It could be a response to the increase of the so-called alternative and independent media they try to distinguish themselves from the mainstream. Boris Ondreička (2017) warns against misuse of the term "alternative," as sometimes extremist ideas and disinformation are presented as an "alternative" to the current democratic constitution.

In the context of funding, the questions related to "independence" present a natural reaction arising from the sensitive nature of the topic of funding. Professional and public events, in which we participated within the research, persuade us to pay attention to the importance of the issue of funding. More and more often, the financial dependence of independent cultural centers is being discussed among laymen and professionals. In the discourse, questions of economical (in)dependence emerge out of (in)dependence of cultural centers on financial funding from the state budget. We realize that questions around funding may often prove to be a sensitive topic. Handling questions of this nature unprofessionally could threaten independent cultural surroundings. An example of unprofessional and ill-considered behavior is the public statement of Michal

Kaščák, the founder and organizer of the biggest Slovak music festival Pohoda.[7] Discussions of funding culture are also held at the parliament. The recent misleading claims against the Audiovizuálny fond (audiovisual fund) by MP Renáta Kaščáková may harm the support of film industry.[8] At the same time, we observe the efforts of political interventions into the work of professional panels,[9] which present a bad signal for the independence of governmental institutions.

In the context of governmental institutions and questions related to the funding of independent cultural centers, one of the most important points is the establishment of the Fond pre podporu umenia[10] (a fund for support of art), or FPU for short. FPU is a government institution supporting art and culture established in 2015. With the establishment of the FPU, came a general change in the financial support of culture in Slovakia. The FPU replaced the majority of the existing grants schemes of the Ministry of Culture. Most importantly, as the first governmental institution, its statues aimed for support and development of independent culture and creative industry. As the first of its kind, it took into consideration the existence and relevance of the environment of the cultural institutions that were not funded by the state. These centers could apply for financial funding in various grant schemes of the Ministry of Culture, the European grant system,

---

7   "I wanted to create an event in a well-funded space of the so-called independent culture. They said they did not feel like doing that as they already ran enough events. They had a secure income and did not try to do anything more. I cannot imagine a club which has to make its own living to react like this. By that. I mean those who can write a good application. Those who make good things, on the other hand, will not get a grant because they have to work on those good things and have no time to fill in the grant forms." BÁLIK, Peter a VYDRA, Anton. Kto bol najlepší minister? In.týždeň, 2018, vol. 15 no. 21, pp. 30–34. ISSN 1136-5932.

8   https://kascakova.blog.sme.sk/c/485083/general-film-storocia-alebo-tunel-storocia.html.

9   https://www.aktuality.sk/clanok/595925/navrat-starych-casov-smer-by-chcel-umelcov-viac-politicky-kontrolovat/.

10  The fund for support of art is established by Law No 284/2014 Coll. On Fund for support of art and amending and supplementing Act No 434/201 Coll. On services within the scope of Ministry of Culture of Slovakia amended by Law No 79/2013 Coll. Of some acts as a public law body for support of artistic activities, culture, and creative industry.

and in schemes of the tertiary sector institutions focusing on supporting art and culture. However, there existed no institution which would consider the fact that the independent cultural centers are an inherent part of the cultural space.

Finances were mostly provided to specific production. In practice, this meant that independent cultural centers could receive funding from multiple grants at once, but also had to bear greater administrative load, i.e. working out and providing statements of the individual projects. The establishment of the FPU should have changed this in a way based on the published appeal so that independent cultural centers would be able to apply for financial support for projects that cover their whole-year activities. By doing this, administrative processes related to working out and providing statements for the project became more effective. It has to be said that the emerging FPU was not aiming to distribute the finances destined for these centers automatically. Already at the early stages of establishing the fund, it was suggested to integrate the finances into the structure of the funding activity.

Independence and professionalism became the main idea behind creating a governmental institution that would act professionally and not intervene with the inner identity of the independent cultural centers when allocating funds for culture and art. The FPU took over the majority of the duties of the Ministry of Culture's existing funding system. However, the whole funding system was not implemented into the fund. Ministry of Culture was still responsible for grants aimed at cultural heritage and support of culture of the disadvantaged population groups. Besides that, FPU, unlike former grant systems of ministry, did not only support and present existing art works, but also aimed to support the actual birth of art. At a press conference held on October 22, 2015, the minister of culture, Marek Maďarič, stated that one of the aims of establishing the FPU was to bring greater financial support for the "non-state" culture. The ambition of the minister was to double the then current package of 10 million euro. In the end, he only managed to increase it by half. Not even a month after the press conference, the FPU published its first appeal. The project organizers of non-commercial art projects in Slovakia, mainly active in the sphere of theater, dance, music, visual art, literature, interdisciplinary cultural activities and folk culture, could submit their applications on January 8,

2016. Among the successful applicants, the FPU planned to divide approximately 2.7 million euro within this first appeal.[11]

The issue of funding independent culture and art leads us to discussion on the role of the FPU in terms of its relation to independent cultural centers in the context of independence or dependence. Moreover, the issue poses questions about the identity of independent culture and art. This is why we focused our research on the analysis of the structure of the funding activity in the first three years of the FPU. The aim was to examine in detail the data about given donations, which are available for public. Another aim was to analyze this data to get a better understanding of the non-state culture funding.

Picture 2

Stanica Žilina-Záriečie

Kultúrne centrum Museum

Klub Lúč

Záhrada - centrum nezávislej kultúry

Tabačka kulturfabrik

Banská Ši a nica

A4 - priestor súčasnej kultúry

Divadlo Pôtoň

In the Picture 2, we can see a map of Slovakia with centers which developed activity in the field of independent culture before 2015, and meanwhile they were authorized to apply for a financial support, which was later granted to them. By marking these on the map of independent cultural centers, we applied the criteria by Anténa – sieť pre nezávislú kultúru (a network for independent culture).[12] Below, we introduce criteria defined by Anténa:[13]

---

11  https://domov.sme.sk/c/8095636/fond-na-podporu-umenia-udeli-prve-dotacie-html

12  Anténa is a network of cultural centers and organizations, which operate in the field of current independent art and culture in Slovakia. www.antenanet.sk.

13  www.antenanet.sk/clenovania.

- they were formed as civil initiatives and are not governed by the state nor municipality,
- their main activity is not performed to gain profit,
- they perform activities continually throughout the whole year and do not organize one-time events only,
- they run a stable venue primarily aimed at organizing activities in the field of independent culture.

In 2016, independent cultural centers could apply for financial support in a sub-program "2.2. Activities of cultural and artistic centers." The support was aimed for subjects that run their activities regularly and connect cultural, artistic, and educational activities. Regarding the structure of the support activities of the above mentioned sub-program, two points represent the conditions for gaining the funding: project's maximum time of verifiable execution period. By the term "project," we mean an independent cultural center. The support of a project was limited to projects lasting for at most five years, which means that in 2016, only those centers could apply for funding that were run since 2010 to 2011 and could verify it. Considering this condition, we may state that the first call was mainly aimed for bigger cultural centers that were formed in the late 90's. For example, Stanica Žilina-Záriečie or A4 – Priestor súčasnej kultúry v Bratislave.

The support structure from 2017 is more detailed in comparison to the first structure from 2016. The individual criteria and conditions are specified in more detail and there are many changes in this structure. One of the changes concerns the priority of support that the Slovak Ministry of Culture gives wherein the ministry declares its support of activities of cultural and artistic centers, and thus provides a place for creating and presenting contemporary art and various cultural activities. Another change is the editing of specific programs and sub-programs mentioned in the structure of support. The most noticeable change, in comparison to the previous year, is the division of the above mentioned sub-program into further two independent sub-programs: 2.2.1 "Activities of bigger cultural and artistic centers" and 2.2.2 "Activities of small and developing cultural and artistic centers." The first sub-program is a support of established independent cultural centers. A proof of this is also a more or less identical list of supported projects from the first two years of funding. The aim of the second mentioned sub-program was to support regional and developing cultural and artistic centers that operate regularly on local or regional level while connecting professional art and cultural activities with educational activities and developing the local cultural and artistic specifics.

In its structure of support, FPU declares that the aim of the sub-program is to support small and developing regional centers that operate on local level. Among the independent cultural and artistic centers projects, we keep a record of small regional centers which were established before the FPU was established and we register developing regional centers that started after 2015, which means after the establishment of FPU. For us, some of the small regional centers formed before 2015 cannot be called truly independent cultural centers in the same way that the well-known bigger established independent cultural centers are called independent. Oftentimes, small centers used to be a good example of an independent center, but because of the regional options and conditions they were forced to seek compromises between the sphere of business and sphere of independent culture and art. The balance between business and distribution of culture required the centers to find space for peripheral formats of art and culture despite the limited options. In their case, an important part of this balance is the afore mentioned inner engagement that starts with the individual and continues up to a group. That is how a specific place maintains its own identity.

The FPU changed the way these small regional cultural and artistic centers were run. Thanks to financial support, some of the centers were free to transform. In the case of gaining support, this meant that the small centers could focus more on the production and dramaturgy of cultural-artistic programs and less on business activities. For example, the music club Wave[14] in Prešov underwent a transformation in 2017. The club changed its name to Wave – Center of Independent Culture and was able to broaden its yearly program and add new dramaturgical elements. On the map of independent cultural centers, Liptovský Mikuláš became more

---

14 www.wave.sk.

important. In a short time, Diera do sveta[15] managed to transform from a bookshop and café to a well-functioning regional independent cultural center. There was also the longest operating space for independent culture in Slovakia: the club Bombura[16] in Brezno. The reason for Bombura not appearing on the map of independent cultural centers earlier is that the possibilities in the region are rather limited. We mention club Bombura, because based on its example we can see the sense of systematic support of small regional cultural and artistic centers. Bombura is still going through stabilization, but we may already state that, peripheral artistic and cultural genres can get into a less-developed region thanks to the gained financial support. It may be said that inner engagement supported this way can influence a larger group of population and hence enrich the region's identity.

We have mentioned centers that were in operation before 2015 and succeeded in gaining financial support during the first call aimed for small and developing cultural and artistic centers. Besides these, we keep a record of centers that started operations after 2015. These centers may be called developing centers. It is the FPU that enabled these developing centers to gain financial support to develop their activities in the field of independent culture. When discussing these centers, we need to take a look at establishment of individual centers in more detail, i.e. examine and analyze factors that influenced their establishment. As in the case of previously established independent cultural centers, the inner engagement and motivation of individuals responsible for a given project should be taken into consideration.

Among the supported projects, Bašta in Bardejov[17] is undoubtedly the most remarkable center. Bašta is a cultural-community center with its seat in the historical tower, which was once a part of the town's fort. Bašta is a natural result of the activities of nonprofit organization Different, the so called "from the bottom" or "self-help" culture. Based on the program structure from the early years of operating, it can be said that Different's aim to build up a cultural-community center has been successful. Regarding

---

15 www.dieradosveta.sk.
16 www.bombura.sk.
17 www.bastakulturnecentrum.sk.

the program structure, it is important to add that we supported the project Rozmanité mesto by the civil association Kandelaber from Bardejov within the call in 2017. It is a civil association closely connected with the civil association Different, which runs Bašta. The civil association Kandelaber does not run any stable venue, so a part of its program has been put into practice in the venues of Bašta, which helps to fulfill the dramaturgical line of the whole program. This cooperation may serve as an example for other small and developing independent cultural centers. In this case, the quest of FPU is to make sure that the supported activities of projects by which such cooperation occurs is clearly separated and charged.

In 2018, there were no remarkable changes observed in the structure of support that would change the character or quest of FPU. We register only small editing changes in definition, conditions and division of programs and sub-programs. In the sub-program 2.2 "Activities of cultural and artistic centers," there is a new classification 2.2.1 "Activities of bigger cultural and artistic centers." In sub-program 2.2.2 "Activities of small cultural and artistic centers," there is now a sub-program 2.2.3 "Activities of residence centers." These new sub-programs are based on an evaluation of specific cultural and artistic centers and the demands of the applicants. Besides this change, we changed the name of the sub-program 2.2.2. The phrase "developing" used in 2017 is no longer in the name. This means that cultural and artistic centers are classified into large and small groups within the structure of supporting activities.

In the sub-program 2.2.1 "Activities of bigger cultural and artistic centers," there were 12 supported projects in 2018, which is the same number as in 2017. From all of the supported projects, 9 of the projects may be marked as independent cultural centers. These projects include: Záhrada – centrum nezávislej kultúry in Banská Bystrica (a center of independent culture), Klub Lúč in Trenčín (a club), Ticho a spol. in Bratislava (a center), Stanica Žilina-Záriečie (a center), Tabačka Kulturfabrik in Košice (a center), Divadlo Pôtoň in Bátovce (a theater), Kultúrne centrum Museum in Martin (a cultural center), and Nová synagóga in Žilina (a synagogue).

If we compare these 9 supported projects, which share the characteristics of independent cultural centers, with the projects from 2017 by applying the same criteria, we find out that the projects are identical. The comparison leads us to the conclusion that after the first three years of FPU, in light of conditions of support, the panel managed to select and recommend the support for projects that are relevant. On the other hand, the supported subjects also proved their relevance by fulfilling the conditions for working out and charging the projects given by the structure of support.

Among the above-mentioned projects sharing the characteristics of independent cultural centers, there are also already established independent cultural centers. As an example, we can point out Záhrada – centrum nezávislej kultúry in Banská Bystrica. Unlike other established centers, Záhrada originated later, in 2010, but within its 8-year existence it managed to equal bigger and more progressive centers. Another early established center is Stanica Žilina-Záriečie, marked as the first independent cultural center, which is often used as an example of an independent cultural center. Moreover, there is another project supported by FPU related to Stanica, Nová synagóga in Žilina. It is a reconstruction project for a neological synagogue that was initiated by the founders Stanica Žilina-Záriečie, Marek Adamov, and Fedor Blaščák. They aimed to not only restore the synagogue but also its life. Thanks to the reconstruction, they created a place for current art and other cultural activities.

In the eastern part of Slovakia, there is an established independent cultural center Tabačka Kulturfabrik. Tabačka Kulturfabrik, which cooperates with Košice municipality, is a rare example of a center focusing on seeking out new economic models of functioning and cooperation between the state and non-state sector. A distinctive center among the established centers is the Divadlo Pôtoň, which is situated in the Slovak countryside in the village of Bátovce. However, its activities cross the regional borders. Regarding the origin, Klub Lúč in Trenčín a Kultúrne centrum Museum in Martin could count as an established independent cultural center. However, if we examine the centers judging by their programs, it has to be said that they are not as progressive as the above-mentioned centers. As the last supported center with characteristics of independent cultural centers, we introduce Ticho a spol., a well-known space for independent theaters in Bratislava, which mainly focuses on theater but also provides space for other art genres.

Regarding the sub-program 2.2.1 "Activities of small cultural and artistic centers," the number of supported projects has grown from 19 to

30 projects. Below, in the picture no. 3, there is a map of Slovakia with marked centers of independent culture which we selected based on our criteria within the analysis of the support in years 2016 up to 2018. The map reflects the state in 2018. In 2016, on the same map, there were 10 established independent cultural centers financially supported in the first call published by FPU. In the third year of the FPU existence, there were 32 spots. This means that in the three years of FPU activity, 22 new spots were added to the map of independent cultural centers. The term spot is used deliberately. Based on broader terminological framework, we cannot call all the new spots proper independent cultural centers. By this, we again want to draw attention to the importance of changing the support structure and broadening of the terminological framework.

**Picture 3**

On the example of smaller regional centers, we can tell that the quest of FPU is mainly to help sustain the independent cultural center in regional conditions. Moreover, in some cases, FPU's quest is to help with the transformation in places where there is less focus on business activities and more attention given to culture and art. In the case of developing centers, the quest of FPU is to give the center a needed impulse to build an independent cultural center by granting them financial support. Activities of some small and developing centers start to be visible in the broader spectrum of independent culture. On the other hand, since the establishment of FPU and the new support of some projects, we begin to keep a record of places and towns where multiple smaller centers operate. An example of this would be the town Martin where in 2018 there were three different cultural centers not cooperating with each other.

Considering the size of the town and region, a question arises: to what extent is it possible to run and financially support three different centers in such a small area. In Banská Bystrica, we register new subjects active in the field of independent culture and art. Unlike in Martin, Záhrada – centrum nezávislej kultúry is a bigger cultural center and actively cooperates with the newly developing cultural-literary center Literárna bašta. Literárna bašta is currently under reconstruction in a new venue, which is why it performs part of its activities in Záhrada. When taking a closer look at the project of Literárna Bašta, it may be expected that the center will specialize with time and thus not compete with Záhrada. If these facts are implemented in the developing centers as a whole, we conclude that a certain part of the centers will, with time, specialize in certain activities and find their place among independent cultural centers. It is likely that not every center will be able to undergo this process and without financial support, some might be forced to close.

## Conclusions

After 2015, questions of economic independence of independent cultural centers came to the forefront. These questions encouraged us to investigate the issue of FPU's quest to support art by financing independent cultural centers in more detail. To verify the stated hypotheses, we focused on the analysis of the support of FPU in its first three years. The reason for the analysis of the 3-year period is the constantly changing form of support structure. In this 3-year period, FPU tried continuously to work with the structure of the support and, at the same time, clearly define its position as an independent governmental institution that supports cultural and artistic environment in the broader grant system of the Slovak republic. To confirm or disprove our hypotheses, we focused on all the projects supported within the analyzed sub-programs. Then, while applying the stated criteria, we divided projects into three groups: projects with the nature of cultural and artistic activities, projects with characteristics of independent cultural centers, and projects in which cultural and artistic activities present a secondary activity. The research confirms the hypothesis that the current structure of support enables to gain financial support for the subjects whose primary activities are neither cultural nor artistic activities. Confirmation of this hypothesis leads us to the problem of terminology. FPU only employs the term *cultural and artistic center*, based on what we distinguish as larger and small cultural and artistic centers. Based on this, we state that the terminological framework of the support structure should be broadened on different terms, upon which it would be possible to derive new sub-programs and criteria.

Based on our research activities, we also state that in the sub-program aimed for larger independent cultural and artistic centers, the established centers succeeded in gaining financial support. This proves their ability to professionalize their activities in the field of art and culture. At the same time, after three years of fund operating, a compact group of bigger cultural centers was formed from the supported projects. On the other hand, the extent of support and activities of individual centers leads us to questions regarding the continual institutionalization and identity threat, wherein the border between "state" and "non-state" begins to be relative. This is based on the fact that some bigger and more established independent cultural centers have to implement new processes, which might lead to continual institutionalization and partial loss of unique identity. In the case of the analysis of the sub-program aimed for small and developing regional centers, we came to a conclusion that the state becomes problematic when the number of submitted applications and supported projects does not correspond with the increase of finances aimed for the support of projects in the mentioned sub-program. The conclusions of the performed analyses lead us to confirm that it is necessary to focus on the issue of institutionalization and sustainability and seek new economic models of functioning of independent cultural centers.

# References:

DANIEL, Ondřej a kol. 2017. *Kultura svépomocí. Ekonomické a politické rozměry v českém subkulturním prostředí pozdního státního socialismu a postsocialismu.* Praha: Filozofická fakulta Univerzity Karlovy.

DUCHOVÁ, Zuzana – KREKOVIČ Slávo. 2017. *BA!! Miesta živej kultúry (1989 – 2016)*. Bratislava: Atrakt.

FROMM, E. 2019. *Anatómia ľudskej deštruktivity*. Bratislava: Citadella.

FUJÁK, Július a kol. *Slovenské hudobné alternatívy*. 1. vyd. Nitra: Univerzita Konštantína Filozofa, 2006, p.125. ISBN 80-8050-944-1.

KNOPOVÁ, Elena. *Súčasné slovenské divadlo v dobe spoločenských premien. Pohľady na slovenské divadlo*. 1. vyd. Bratislava: Veda, 2017, p. 368. ISBN 978-80-22-41-620-7.

**Newspapers and Journals**

ONDREIČKA, Boris. *Alternatívne prebudenie sa*. In Kapitál, 2018, roč. 1. č. 2, pp. 8–9. ISSN 2585-7851.

**Online Sources**

Web 1. Štruktúra podpornej činnosti na rok 2016. Available online: http://www.fpu.sk/attachments/article/84/STRUKTURA_FPU_final.pdf.

Web 2. Štruktúra podpornej činnosti na rok 2017. Available online: http://www.fpu.sk/attachments/article/84/STRUKTURA%20 2017_08022017_3.pdf.

Web 3. Štruktúra podpornej činnosti na rok 2018. Available online: http://www.fpu.sk/attachments/article/84/STRUKTURA%20 2018_08012018.pdf.

Lucia Kurpašová

The Department of Culture and Tourism Management,
Faculty of Arts, Constantine the Philosopher University
in Nitra

# Identity and Culture in a Tourist Destination on the Example of Village Ždiar

**Abstract:** The aim of this contribution is to describe the influence tourism has on traditional culture in the characteristic village Ždiar. We focus on the functional transformation of traditional culture and its purpose in tourism. This contribution deals with the forms of cultural heritage and analyses of the competitive advantages of the use of cultural heritage in local culture. A further aim is to investigate the effects of tourism on local culture. This article focuses on the output of research dedicated to traditional culture of ski-centers.

**Keywords:** Identity, authenticity, traditional culture, culture heritage.

## Introduction

Since requirements are increasing and population is growing quickly, cultural heritage is one of the most endangered and non-renewable sources. In response to the current trends in tourism, managers, providers, and the self-government agencies are forced to make decisions that have the potential to negatively influence the quality of the local cultural heritage. Globalization, urbanization, and multiculturalism are main culprits in this negative influence since they disturb the authenticity of individual localities.

The contribution aims to point out the influence of civilization on tourism that positively and negatively affects the identity of contemporary inhabitants. We aim to research the transformation of culture from its traditional state to its current version. We will evaluate its importance for the development of tourism, specifically in pursuit of a better way to preserve the identity and authenticity of the researched tourist destination. We want to research the influence tourism has on local inhabitants and culture at the local level. We also want to explore the effects of the decisions of the former inhabitants, who are often perceived as competition, on traditional culture.

We have measured whether the original cultural traditions of the village are presented to visitors. We have explored whether or not modern or the so-called "mass" elements of transformed character are preferred, since the authenticity of a destination changes the offer and suppresses their cultural identity.

The research was conducted in 2017 and 2018 in the form of interviews and both active and passive observation. The representatives of local self-governments, owners of accommodation facilities, the workers at ski-resorts, and development organizations served as informants. Moreover, we used the statistical data of the local government. We analyzed and generalized the material received from respondents.

We focus on naming key factors of culture formation in Ždiar. They are determinants of cultural heritage and identity of village inhabitants. We will note the elements creating competitiveness of the destination and limiting factors that may disturb the authenticity of the village.

## Ždiar

The traditional culture of the village Ždiar is one of the most preserved in Slovakia. It is situated 32 km north of the town Poprad. The cadastral area is 2733 ha and the adjoining area is located at an altitude of 820–2146 m.a.s.l. The village lies in Podtatranská trench, borders with Spišská Magura from the north, Eastern Tatras from the east, and state border with Poland (13 km) from the west. The southern border is comprised of the High and Belianske Tatras between Rysy and Tatranská Kotlina. Wide saddle divides Belianske Tatras into two parts. The western part has two significant peaks: Ždiarska Vidla (2142 m.a.s.l.) and the highest mountain Havran (2152 m.a.s.l.) The second part is comprised of the most western peak Muráň. There are no similar areas in Slovakia with regards to nature conservation. There is a variety of flora, phytogeographic significant species, and specific relief. The whole adjoining area is a part of the protected area of TANAP (Tatra National Park). This is the area richest in flora and fauna. It is a locality of a European significance. In 1991, the area of 5408 ha was declared a National Nature Reserve Belianske Tatry. It also belongs to the nature reserve Goliasová, UNESCO, and the individual parts of the village were declared as monuments reserve in 1977 (PRĽA – Monument Reserve of Folk architecture) (KOLLÁROVÁ et al. 2013: 6–15).

Despite the difficult climate, Ždiar has been inhabited since the beginning of the second half of the sixteenth century. The first written notice of the village is from 1590. However, based on the Vlach law, the village was formerly inhabited much earlier. When isolated mountain hamlets were established, lands were divided in such a way that the village estate was separated into similar parts, the so-called *zárubky*. According to the number of the settlers, the settler could build a house only within their part. Village Ždiar is unique in its folk architecture, which was influenced by the Goral culture. The former inhabitants were mostly peasants, herdsmen, charcoal burners, and woodcutters.

Village Ždiar has currently more than 1300 inhabitants. The village is nicely situated near the Polish border close to a significant route, Poprad (SVK) – Zakopane (PL), which has helped it to become a dynamic and modern village (*Pamiatková rezervácia ľudovej architektúry v Ždiari – Urbanisticko-historický výskum* 2017: <https://www.pamiatky.sk/Content/ZASADY/Zdiar/0101–Zdiar-u-hi-vyskum.pdf>).

## The Specifics of Cultural Formation in the Village Ždiar

The culture of Slovak villages was formed by many coincidences. It was the product of natural and climate conditions and the administrative division of the country. Moreover, there were ethnic and confessional factors, migration flows, colonization, and other historical events. The surrounding villages and local cultural centers also influenced the culture. Moreover, local inhabitants played a very important role. All of these factors are represented in the art, folk costumes, religious culture, and folklore (BEŇUŠKOVÁ et al. 2005: 15–25).

According to the Slovak regionalization, Ždiar belongs to the eastern Slovak mountain culture of the Carpathians and the cultural region Spiš. The Spiš region extends into the north-eastern part of Slovakia near the basins Popradská and Hornádska, and the valley of Hnilec with the adjoining mountain ranges. The region is bordered by the High Tatras from the west, Spišská Magura from the north, the Levoča mountains and Branisko from the south, and it also partially belongs into the Slovak Ore

**Figure 1** Village Ždiar
**Source:** Lucia Kurpašová (Ždiar, August 2018)

Mountains. The whole region is mostly mountainous (BEŇUŠKOVÁ et al. 2005: 173).

Historically, Spiš is divided into upper and lower parts. It is divided according to how the Poprad and Hornád rivers flow. The village Ždiar belongs to the upper Spiš bordered by Belianske Tatras, which played a significant role in the formation of the village. The Belianske Tatras were inhabited mostly by the Ruthenian and Goral shepherds, who created the original folk architecture and art. The colonization of the mountainous region of Spiš was based on the Vlach law from the fifteenth–sixteenth century. The inhabitants of the Goral and Ruthenian villages earned their living farming cattle and sheep at sheepcote farms. Poor geographical and climate conditions made for infertile soil, which in turn brought about the development of sheep and cattle farming. The Gorals form the greater part of 34 villages set in two regions: the north one which is compact, and the south one, the valley of Poprad river. Ždiar is a characteristic Goral village. The Gorals differ from the rest of the inhabitants by their dialect and material culture – clothes, architecture and folklore. The Gorals in northern parts of the Spiš region are adherents of the Roman Catholic Church (BEŇUŠKOVÁ et al. 2005: 174–175).

The first wave of emigration of the subjects from the northern Slovakia was caused by the disadvantageous climate, the subsequent economic crisis, and inability to cope with the former regulations from territorial lords and public regulations between 1715–1716. The subsequent emigration from 1884 to 1889 influenced life in the village. The inhabitants mostly left for work in the USA. The emigration was caused by buying up pledged fertile lands. In the end of the twentieth century, the village was influenced by the tourism that became the main source of the revenues for a lot of the local inhabitants (*Pamiatková rezervácia ľudovej architektúry v Ždiari – Urbanisticko-historický výskum* 2017: <https://www.pamiatky.sk/Content/ZASADY/Zdiar/0101–Zdiar-u-hi-vyskum.pdf>).

Demographics and the composition of the population demonstrate the current social development of the village. Regarding the demography, there are significant trends in decreasing births and the ageing of the population. However, in the case of Ždiar, the number of permanent inhabitants is on the rise. Recently, the village population has increased because of an influx of new inhabitants who were not born in the village but moved there. Moreover, the ratio of men and women is balanced. The number of inhabitants (according to the Statistical office research from 2014) of Ždiar is 1382, 680 of which were men and 702 women.

Based on the data from the Statistical office, the structure of employment in the village Ždiar in 2011 was as follows. Most inhabitants worked in the agricultural sector, wholesale and retail, industry, construction industry, accommodation and catering services. This data reflects the conditions and locality of village Ždiar and what the village can offer to the inhabitants and visitors. Since the second half of the twentieth century, the inhabitants of village Ždiar have been employed mostly thanks to opportunities in the tourism sector, which is the biggest source of revenues in this foothill village. Inhabitants are mostly employees or owners of accommodation facilities. Another group of inhabitants conduct business in forestry or are employed as workmen in the forest. Others commute to

the surrounding towns for employment (Poprad, Tatranská Lomnica, etc.)
(*Program hospodárskeho rozvoja a sociálneho rozvoja obce Ždiar na roky
2015–2022* 2015: <http://staryweb.zdiar.sk/images/stories/_schvalene_
dokumenty/PHSR%202015–2022.pdf>).

## Traditional Culture and Identity Formation

Until the 1950s, the village was the dominant source of religious and material culture within Slovakia. The people preserved family customs related
to *birth of a child, christening, maturing, wedding* and strictly followed
the rituals related to *death and funeral.* (KOLLÁROVÁ et al. 2013: 140).
In our text, we focus mostly on the traditions that are used in tourism.

The *common family traditions* that have been preserved the best are
traditions related to the pre-wedding time of engaged couples. In the
past, engaged couples had to go through the banns three times before the
wedding day. Nowadays, they must do it only once. Banns are held on a
Sunday before the wedding and are called "kuliky." During the banns,
the future married couple arrives to the church wearing traditional folk
costumes. This is now rare in modern-day Slovakia. The traditions that
come after are related to the leaving of the groom and bride to the church,
parents' blessing, and taking the bride from her native home. The common
traditions related to the arrival to a new house and putting the bonnet
on the head of the bride called "čepčenie" ritual have the same authenticity. During the banns and čepčenie ritual, the newly married couple
and wedding guests wear the original wedding folk costumes of Ždiar
(BUDZÁKOVÁ 2017).

Regarding the family customs, first communion ceremony has been preserved. All children in the third grade of the primary school, their parents,
godparents, and grandparents enter the church in local folk costumes. This
is the most favorite ceremony among tourists.

There are also calendar customs. Here we will cover mostly those
related to *spring* and *winter time.* Specifically, people preserve the Palm
Sunday and the Easter time traditions. Nowadays, the Easter customs like
water pouring and whipping have taken on a modern character adopted
from western Slovak regions which is not authentic of Ždiar. Easter is cel-
ebrated mostly in the church. The inhabitants of Ždiar come to the mass in

traditional folk costumes. Locals come to church on Palm Sunday to bless the food. During Easter in Ždiar, it is usual to "stand guard at the tomb of Jesus." Adult men and their sons take turns and stand by the tomb of Jesus together (BURGEROVÁ 2017).

Another preserved spring custom is *putting up the maypole*. However, the maypoles are not put up on the first of May. Instead, people do it during Pentecost, which is the holiday that was once most significant annual holiday in the pre-Christian era. The pupils of the primary school put up the maypole, usually in front of the school.

During winter and pre-Christmas season, people celebrate St. Nicholas day in the form of a mass in church and at Christmas, they tree lit afterwards. During Christmas, boys from the village and the local children ensemble Ždiaranček gathers and goes carolling with the Nativity scene. They sing Christmas songs and go down the village on Christmas Eve, New Year's Day, and Epiphany. On Christmas Eve, inhabitants and tourists can attend the midnight mass. On Christmas Day, there is a mass held at the Church of the Visitation in Ždiar. People can enjoy there carols, a live Nativity scene and some refreshments. This accompanying event is organized by the citizen's association Spolok dedičstva goralov with children ensemble Ždiaranček in collaboration with the sponsors Kamzík guest house, Aja guest house, Wellness Guest House Strachan ***, Hotel Bachledka Strachan ****, Hotel Magura**.

Traditional St. Stephen's parties are not organized institutionally in the village, but individually by hoteliers in the individual accommodation facilities. The same situation occurs on New Year's Eve and New Year's Day celebrations. Events on both days are held individually in the accommodation facilities. Due to the environmental and forest protection efforts, fireworks have been prohibited in the village for several years. The ethnic variety of the inhabitants of Ždiar can been seen in their architecture, clothing and textiles, and the Goral dialect and songs that are still alive. Ždiar's folklore is influenced by the Spiš and Podhradie regions, where Goral music (violin and bass) with authentic dance is popular. The song and dance are dynamic and features "rozkazovačky" (commands), men brigand's dances, original shepherd performances or funny tag called "Kotka." During slow wedding dances, "Rovny" dance is the most suitable.

Folklore fans who make up the authentic folklore group Goral try to implement the original folk dances and rituals into their program. The group often performs during the Goral Folklore Festival that began in 1994. The folklore festival is a form of preserving the intangible cultural heritage of Ždiar. Folklorists of all ages present traditions and culture of this region. The folklore festival takes place during two concurrent days with more than 200 performers. The event takes place at the foot of Ždiarska Vidla and Havran mountains in the premises of Ski center Strednica a.s. The festival regularly starts with a Catholic mass on both days. The locals always attend the festival wearing traditional folk costumes. The Ždiar festival has been the most visited event in Ždiar for several years (BUDZÁKOVÁ 2017, BURGEROVÁ 2017, MICHALÁKOVÁ 2017, ZORIČÁKOVÁ 2018).

Genres of the original folk literature in Ždiar mirror the way of living in the mountain area. For village inhabitants, folk poetry was very important. It was created during work at home, land, in the forest and during the ordinary life of the inhabitants.

The people's way of living in Ždiar was significantly present in the specific local folk costumes. These costumes enabled people to differ from others. The clothes had mostly protective function against disadvantageous climate conditions. The inhabitants characterize Ždiar's climate as quite cold, reporting that "winter lasts here twelve months, the rest of the year is warm." The basic materials used were leather, fur, bark, wood, juniper's roots, canvas, and broadcloth. Linen canvas was traditional material. After the reforms of Maria Theresa, silk fabrics were introduced. The clothes became colorful and more decorative using mostly half-silk brocade, silk velour, and tibet (KOLLÁROVÁ et al. 2013: 132–133).

Goral and Ruthenian inhabitants differed from German inhabitants in that they made use of green and red fabrics. These colors were also dominant in home interiors. The folk costumes of Ždiar share many elements with Goral villages in the Orava region. The men's folk costume predominately includes white trousers from broadcloth, the so-called "portki" decorated with blue-red string. The costume also includes a vest called "serdok" made from sheep's leather, which is brown on the outside and richly embroidered with "makov." The hats are decorated with shells and a feather, which the most characteristic piece of the ensemble. This costume is one of the most popular souvenirs the High Tatras offers.

The women's folk costume has different variations than the men's. It consists of a wide-sleeved shirt and bodice that is connected to the underskirt. The underskirt is girded to the black upper skirt, the edge of which is decorated with white lace. Women also wear festive costumes with white skirts. Married women used to wear richly decorated bonnets, e.g. with tip and forehead covered with scarf. The Spiš bonnets were generally divided into so-called "Russian," "Catholic," and "Polish" bonnets (BURGEROVÁ 2017, KOLLÁROVÁ et al. 2013: 134).

The original use of traditional folk costume is preserved today but in a limited way. Nowadays, traditional folk costumes are used mostly as festive costumes. Men and women wear them at all significant events – christening, first communion, wedding, ball, funeral, and during more

**Figure 2** Mass – Opening of the second day of Goral Folklore Festival 2018
**Source:** Lucia Kurpašová (Ždiar, 2018)

significant calendar holidays, e.g. when visiting church – Easter, Christmas, etc. (ZORIČÁKOVÁ 2018).

Folk architecture is the most significant element of traditional culture in Ždiar. The living arrangements of the inhabitants were heavily influenced by the difficult climate conditions. Forests were gradually deforested. Obtaining pasture lands was so difficult that shepherds were forced to settle in the improvised single-room wooden shepherd's huts. In the beginnings of the nineteenth century, agrarian hamlets were established in several parts of the current form of the village (KOLLÁROVÁ et al. 2013: 128–129). Log cabins that created atria along with farming buildings remain in Ždiar. The yard behind the longer part of the house was surrounded by farming buildings. The barn in the rear part of the yard stood parallel to the house and the rest of the smaller farm materials were at the sides of the yard. Wood was the basic building material and the whole structure had log cabin character (KOLEKTÍV 1998: 313).

Those who owned new houses positioned their homes so that the living space would face the sun with their farm buildings in sight. Main farm buildings were built opposite the residential house toward the north. The people also took care to decorate their log cabins in the authentic style of Ždiar. Gables of houses were carved in various shapes. The gables also contained symbols of stylized edelweiss, silver thistle etc. The outer decoration was oriented mostly at the front façade. Besides the strong angle bonds, planks around the windows and typical shingled roof, the wooden houses in Ždiar had a specific style. Modern grouting of logs and greasing of edges contrasts with the patina of the wood and shingle (BEŇUŠKOVÁ 2005: 177–176, KOLLÁROVÁ et al. 2013: 130–131).

At present, we can find two different log cabin layouts in Ždiar. There is one that is characteristic of Ždiar, with asymmetrical premises and the "Polish" one characteristic of Zakopane with the entrance hall located in the middle of the layout. The original color of the built-up area was underlined by the light blue coating with the moss, gaps between logs grouted with clay in the dwelling area, and red window frames were supplemented by the simple white ornament. At present, the village has 183 national cultural heritage monuments.

**Figure 3** Traditional architecture in Ždiar – hill Antošovský vrch, part of PRĽA
Source: Lucia Urbanová (Ždiar, 2017)

## Current Situation and the Influence of Civilization and Cultural Processes on the Identity and Traditional Culture

In 1932, the film *Zem spieva* (Singing country) directed by Karol Plicka was released. The film had an important role in the preservation and promotion of Ždiar, and eventually also played a role in the subsequent changes of traditional local culture and identity of Ždiar. In his film, the director showed many characteristic elements of the authentic culture village, including folklore, notes on the specific dialect, songs, and the traditional folk costumes. The promotion brought a number of tourists to the region. In the middle of the nineteenth century, many tourists, mostly from Poland, visited the area. Tourists from Germany visited as well. There were 5 guests who visited the village in 1928, 30 guests came on vacation in 1930, and more than 100 guests visited the village in 1932. Due to the insufficient capacities, 70 guests had to be rejected. In 1933, 285 tourists visited the village, 21 of which were from abroad (KOLLÁROVÁ et al. 2013: 48). In the end of the twentieth century, the increasing tourism influenced the village so much that it became the main source of income for many local inhabitants.

The more tourists visited the village, the less locals wore traditional costumes and started to get used to city elements. This was not only an effect of tourism but also of the migration of local inhabitants to other regions for work. In the following years, the situation became so serious that the traditional Goral folk costume almost vanished from the ordinary life of the inhabitants.

In 1974, a priest named Ľudovít Šlepecký started working in the village. His interest in traditions resulted in a folk costume renaissance and the customs of celebrating important events in traditional folk costume were renewed. Liturgical year ceremonies, First Communion, christening, confirmation, banns, weddings, were all revived according to the traditions of old. The restoration of folk costumes was very difficult after years of not being utilized. By this time, the original inhabitants who knew how to make them had almost disappeared from the village, and the original manufacturing elements had to be collected from museum records (ZORIČÁKOVÁ 2018). Now, the traditional and authentic costumes are the pride of Ždiar. It is a phenomenon that is a part of the cultural character of the locality and allows tourists to connect with the original culture.

The increased number of visitors intensified the development of the village, mostly in residential areas. This fact significantly influenced traditional physical environment, mostly with regards to architecture. The inhabitants of Ždiar changed layouts of many houses, reconstructed, and adapted them for the sake of tourism. Sometimes, these changes were at the expense of historical and architectural tradition. Several studies were made in the past in an effort to reconstruct the village in a way that preserved the character of the original Goral village. Many proposals were approved but have never been finished. The project to restore the architecture to the original characteristic folk style finally did take off, resulting in the announcement of Folk architecture reservation in Ždiar in three parts of the village: western – the Upper end, eastern part and valleys – Bachledova dolina and Blaščacká dolina and hill Antošovský vrch. There are currently 183 national cultural heritage monuments that are parts of historic zones (*Pamiatková rezervácia ľudovej architektúry v*

*Ždiar – Urbanisticko-historický výskum* 2017: <https://www.pamiatky. sk/Content/ZASADY/Zdiar/0101–Zdiar-u-hi-vyskum.pdf>). Later, Ždiar developed rules to govern the reconstruction and construction of village buildings. The basic standards are to be followed not only in historic zones, but in the whole village. The Monuments Board governs the historic zones and approves the construction pursuant to the specifically stipulated standards, which e.g. highlight the need of constructing from the instructed material that is hard to find nowadays. These materials include wood and "Ždiar stone" that was used for lining of the foundation wall. Nowadays, it is difficult to find and harvest due to environmental changes. The stone shall be used solely from the village cadastre, mining of which is nowadays impossible. Deposits are in the protected areas where the mining is prohibited (DOYLE 2018, PITOŇÁK 2018).

The materials required for the construction of houses include Goral elements from the Polish border architecture (e.g. house with several floors – Strachan guest house etc.) that do not have much in common with the traditional architectural elements of Ždiar. We agree with Vaníček (2008, p. 6) and emphasize that after the event of declaring the village a folk architecture reservation, it was assumed that the village would be visible on tourist maps. In our opinion, this fact has a small role in Ždiar tourism, mostly regarding the present massive construction of small accommodation facilities that do not correspond with the elements of traditional construction. The main problem is that the former inhabitants interested in the preservation of cultural character are not the only owners and operators of the real estate and accommodation facilities. Destination managers, self-government representatives, businessmen, and inhabitants of Ždiar admit that it is easier to pay the penalty to the Building Office and Monuments Board for possible final approval of the object than to follow the standards (BURGEROVÁ 2017, DOYLE 2018, MICHALÁKOVÁ 2018, PITOŇÁK 2018).

The village tried to implement mass regulations for the construction and reconstruction of real estates also in non-historic zones, but the inhabitants did not like it because of the illegal actions of the self-government. There is little overall cooperation between the self-government and the inhabitants. On the one hand, the inhabitants point out that the village is not interested in this matter enough and that it does not cooperate.

They mostly emphasize the lack of material support when organizing cultural life in Ždiar. On the other hand, the village regards the behavior of inhabitants in the matter of tax duties as incorrect. From the viewpoint of the self-government, the inhabitants do not give real number of visitors to avoid paying accommodation tax per tourist. This is only one example of negative factors influencing the budget of the village.

There are also problems with the organization of cultural events in the village, particularly with the most visited *Goral Folklore Festival*. The organization of a two-day event has its limits. On the first day, only the mass and evening party are planned, of which only local inhabitants have been informed. The actual festival starts on the second day. The inhabitants and tourists have noticed short timing of the festival. The space in which the festival is held is one of the main organizational problems. The festival used to take place at the ski center Strednica a.s. The resort does not have single owner, but it is governed by the principle of land associations. However, each owner of the land is not its shareholder and many of the owners are not interested in the center's condition. Those interested in making the economy of the center better and to put measures in place to do so, do not have enough votes. The attempt of the village to construct a permanent amphitheater in Strednica center that would serve during the whole year and adequately substitute the absent community center, has not been approved due to nearby terrain. Another problem of the festival is the insufficient labor to cover the work involved in an event of this size (MICHALÁKOVÁ 2018).

In the past, the festival was once organized in the valley Monkova near the hotel Magura, but the parking lots capacity was insufficient for the number of cars, which forced the organizers to move the festival to Strednica.

After the opening of the treetop walk *Chodník korunami stromov* in autumn 2017, the number of tourists visiting Ždiar has increased. According to Dušan Šiška, general manager of ski center Bachledka Ski&Sun, the opening caused a big increase in tourists in just several days. The walk opened in the first week of September and as of November 24, 2017, it has been visited by 75 000 visitors. The biggest number of visits was recorded during the third weekend when 7000 visitors came on one day. The following seasons will likely bring an even bigger number of tourists. The operation can be covered thanks to the full reconstruction of the cable way that shall provide bigger transport capacity per hour (the former conditions enabled 350 people per hour, now it should be more than 1000 people per hour) (ŠIŠKA 2017).

The lack of sufficient parking brought the village extreme traffic congestion. The owner of the ski center Bachledka Ski & Sun tried to solve the situation by constructing new parking lots. The center also constructed a new cable way that was officially put into operation in the beginning of the winter season 2018/2019 (PAVLÍKOVSKÝ 2018).

The owner plans to open a new accommodation and catering facility, which Ždiar currently lacks. Currently, the superstructure is excessively overloaded. There is very little traditional cuisine. Instead of local specialties, almost all the restaurants offer visitors universal menus containing elements of international cuisine. Another weakness is that a tourist has nowhere to eat after 21:00. Considering the massive visits to the center, it is a big paradox.

People visiting Ždiar can find accommodations in 29 guest houses, 31 lodgings, 16 chalets, and two hotels. These accommodation facilities have the capacity of around 3000 beds (*Ubytovanie* 2017: <http://zdiar. sk/navstevnik/ubytovanie/>). The current situation is changing. During tourist season (summer and winter), there are no vacancies and the accommodation facilities are fully occupied, which motivates the construction of new accommodation facilities. According to the operators, there is still a lack of sufficient accommodation during peak tourist season. Each year, there are new accommodation facilities built in the village (DOYLE 2017). However, only a minority of them respects traditional local architecture, despite being located directly in historic zones.

## Cultural Heritage of Ždiar and Tourism

The increase in tourism during the twentieth century brought about a need to revert back to the original way of living in Ždiar. In 1971, the village established the House of Ždiar (Ždiarsky dom) with a museum that stands there to this day. The object was constructed according to the samples of the former wooden houses from 1911 and 1914. The construction was separated into two parts: residential and farming. The residential part of the construction houses is a permanent exhibition of the typical interior of the time. There are work tools, agricultural tools, typical furniture of the house, various folk costumes, toys, pets, and musical instruments known in the northern Spiš and Podhradie in Poland. There is also a famous violin "zlobcoky" made by the local artist Matej Pitoňák in Ždiar. The exhibition is constantly supplemented with new exhibits due to the increasing development of tourism.

The farming part contains the restaurant that since 1973 has been a huge contribution to the economy of the village, since there were once much fewer catering facilities in Ždiar back then. In order to be more authentic, the staff wear stylized working costumes native to Ždiar called "šohajdy" *(Múzeum Ždiarsky dom Ždiar* 2017: <http://www.muzeum. sk/?obj=muzeum&ix=mzdd>).

The current main task of the museum is to collect and preserve physical heritage of the village and to present the intangible one. In the past, the museum was rented to a private entrepreneur, but this caused stagnation of the object for a while so as of the first half of 2017, the museum belongs to the newly established citizens' association named OZ Spolok goralského dedičstva, which is managed by MA Katarína Burgerová.

The exhibit that draws the biggest attention to the museum is the traditional Ždiar wedding re-enactment. Visitors are invited to participate in an imitation of a Ždiar wedding according to the original traditions. Some time ago, the original wedding ceremony notes were found. The wedding ceremonies were once performed according to the notes and are now used during these re-enactments.

During the imitation wedding, the participants, including the bride, groom, best man, bridesmaid and priest, wear traditional Ždiar folk costumes available for rent. The wedding is often adjusted depending on the specific group of visitors. The bride and groom exchange prop wedding rings made of wire, which they can keep, and the museum issues them souvenir marriage certificate. After the wedding, the "newly-weds" go for a ride on a horse-drawn carts typical for this ceremony. A team of horses takes them along the local surroundings of the village and leaves them in front of the restaurant, where they are invited to taste the local specialties and traditional beverages. Several elements are adopted from the other side of the Tatras from Polish Gorals (BUDZÁKOVÁ 2017, BURGEROVÁ 2017, VOJTAŠÁKOVÁ 2018, ZORIČÁKOVÁ 2018).

The aim is that by participating in the re-enactment, the tourists experience a sample of what an authentic Goral wedding of Ždiar is like with all the original elements. The wedding is presented in modified and humorous way, but it allows the participants to experience the original way of living at least partially. All of the different elements add to the experience, from the clothes and songs, to the ride through village on horse-drawn carts.

The fundamental element for successful protection of village culture is including cultural heritage in tourism. The necessary component in this process is a shared vision by the community and contributing members of the local economy. This shared outlook offers a basic openness to the attempt and allows for the development of partnerships and public participation.

Moreover, if the village is to successfully preserve their culture through tourism, is it necessary to erect permanently sustainable tourism destinations? Tourism is an important part of preserving, promoting, and developing the cultural heritage of a village. Tourism plays an important role in constructing awareness of the universal value of cultural heritage in the given locality. Field representatives should be increasingly aware of the significance of cultural heritage and its potential to protect and coordinate the development of destinations. Moreover, they should help managers and marketers solve problems. Support of tourism representatives means support for protection attempts. It changes politics of cooperating subject; therefore, it motivates visitors to contribute to the preservation of cultural heritage and identity.

The promotion of the real image of the locality, informing about attempts of coordinated development, education about minimizing visitors' influence, and provisions about contribution to the locality protection belong into the important elements of new development plans. When managers, marketers, and all subjects participating in the locality understand and value the chain of tourism and cultural heritage, they gain a tool to identify obstacles and reach compromises in the event of conflicts of interest. Only then are they able to use these opportunities to create a better experience for the visitors and create a multiplication effect. Tourism connected to cultural heritage has difficulty with the information, knowledge, and understanding of cultural values of locality and problems emerging from the management of destination. Moreover, it must meet the current travelling trends and tourist expectations. This data is the key for the development of efficient entry points for cooperation and coordination between tourism, culture management, and local development activities. Partnerships in the field of tourism develop creative mechanisms with potential to get funds for the protection of cultural heritage locality. The area declared as the cultural heritage locality makes businessmen and self-government support steps that increase promotion of culture of the locality and provide the development pursuant to the protection of the tourism offer (KURPAŠ – ZIMA 2016: 147–148). Reciprocity, protection of cultural heritage, and its preservation and use within the context of tourism is a worldwide trend contributing to the attractiveness of the destination and creating a complex touristic experience, while at the same time preserving the identity of local inhabitants.

## Conclusions

The current appearance of tourist destinations is related to their continuous development. The primary natural conditions that influenced the way of living of local inhabitants and physical and intangible culture through which the region and its inhabitants may be identified and presented have the most important role during destination formation.

Besides the attractive nature, quality sport centers and various attractions, Ždiar offers peculiar and authentic traditional culture even today. It is characterized by Goral dialect, traditional cuisine, traditional architecture, rich variations of folk costumes and mostly specific and unique folklore. The authenticity of the locality is a phenomenon and competitive factor in tourism.

Two main aspects detrimental to the development of the village are weak promotion and insufficient presentation of competitive advantages. The lack of cooperation between local institutions and tourism subjects is another weakness. Nevertheless, quality destination management may balance the preservation and efficient use of traditional culture in tourism in this locality. Self-government points out that they miss the erudite management that could solve this problem directly. It also highlights the need of expanding cooperation with inhabitants to a wider extent. Not only Zelenka (2010: 174–175) considers the improvement of the image of local events an important part of destination marketing. Weak promotion of events does not improve the situation but rather stresses ineffective use of funds. Pompurová (2014: 204–205) mentions that the coordination and promotion of the organized events shall be provided by the village on the local level and by the regional tourism organization on the wider level. We also agree with this statement. However, the reality is often different. Economic power of many self-governments does not enable them to employ professionals responsible for specific fields (in this case marketing, i.e. tourism), i.e. employees of municipal authorities do not have enough time to solve issues of destination marketing.

The presented civilizational impacts explained in detail in the previous articles negatively influence the local culture that indirectly adapts to tourists and thus loses its originality. Insufficient use of cultural offer within tourism may be explained by the inadequate level of cooperation between the subjects operating in the locality.

Similar approach to researching mutual influence of traditional culture and tourism will be applied in other destinations in Slovakia. The outputs of the analysis will be mutually compared with an aim to point out the ways and meaning of using traditional culture in tourism that consequently supports competitiveness of the destination.

Formation of collective identities during the modern period happened at the backdrop of various events with different causes and consequences. Despite all the influences and ongoing cultural transformation in tourist destinations and regarding the current state of the village we may say that local inhabitants still preserve the identity of Goral inhabitants.

# References:

BEŇUŠKOVÁ, Z. et al. *Tradičná kultúra regiónov Slovenska. Prehľad charakteristických znakov.* Bratislava: SAV, 2005. 262 p. ISBN 80–224–0518–3.

KOLLÁROVÁ, Z. et al. *Dedičstvo Goralov, Ždiar.* Ždiar: Obec Ždiar, 2013, p. 175. ISBN 978-80-970944-7-8.

KOLEKTÍV, *Ľudová architektúra a urbanizmus vidieckych sídiel na Slovensku.* Bratislava: Academic Electronic Press, 1998, p. 360. ISBN 80-88880-23-8.

KURPAŠ, M. – ZIMA, R. Manažment a marketing kultúrneho dedičstva In: *Kultúrne dedičstvo a identita / zborník z vedeckej konferencie konanej v Banskej Bystrici 25–26 May 2016.* Banská Bystrica: Belianum, 2016. – ISBN 978-80-557-1120-1, pp. 145–154.

*Múzeum Ždiarsky dom Ždiar (House of Ždiar).* [online]. 2000 – 2017 [quoted 2018–01–28]. Available online: <http://www.muzeum.sk/?obj=muzeum&ix=mzdd>

*Pamiatková rezervácia ľudovej architektúry v Ždiari – Urbanisticko-historický výskum* [online]. 2008 – 2009. [quoted 2017-20-2017]. Available online: <https://www.pamiatky.sk/Content/ZASADY/Zdiar/0101-Zdiar-u-hivyskum.pdf> POMPUROVÁ, K. Nevyhnutnosť koordinácie ponuky organizovaných podujatí na Slovensku. In *Ekonomická revue cestovného ruchu.* 2014, year 47, issue no. 4, pp. 196–206.

*Program hospodárskeho rozvoja a sociálneho rozvoja obce Ždiar na roky 2015–2022.* [online] 2015 [quoted 2018-05-19]. Available online: <http://staryweb.zdiar.sk/images/stories/_schvalene_dokumenty/PHSR%202015-2022.pdf>. VANÍČEK, J. Význam vesnických památkových rezervací a zón v České republice pro rozvoj obcí z hlediska cestovního ruchu. In *Ekonomická revue cestovného ruchu.* 2008, year 41, issue no. 1, pp. 5–13.

*Ubytovanie.* [online] 2017 [quoted 2018-01-30]. Available online: <http://zdiar.sk/navstevnik/ubytovanie/>.

**List of Informants:**

BACHLEDOVÁ, Iveta. *Operator – Wellness Guest House Strachan* * * *: 2017.

BEKEŠ, Pavol. *Mayor of village Ždiar:* 2017.

BUDZÁKOVÁ, Monika. *Museum – House of Ždiar:* 2017.

BURGEROVÁ, Katarína. *Director OZ Spolok Goralského dedičstva:* 2017 DOYLE, Ivana. *Owner of accommodation facility Belianska Chata:* 2017 KARŠŇÁK, Milan (1955) – KARŠŇÁKOVÁ, Jana (1959). *Visitors of the village:* 2018.

MAČÁKOVÁ, Martina. – MAČÁK, Peter. *Owners of the accommodation facility Piero in Ždiar:* 2017.

MICHALÁKOVÁ, Blanka. *Municipal authority – Village development*: 2017.

STRIŠOVSKÁ, Jana. *Operator of the accommodation facility and ski center Magura in valley Monková*: 2017.

PAVLÍKOVSKÝ, Emil (1972) – PAVLÍKOVSKÁ, Monika (1974). Inhabitants of village, operator of cableway at the ski center Bachledka Ski & Sun: 2018.

PITOŇÁK, Miroslav (1963). Inhabitant of village, founder of the ensemble Ždiaranček, operator of cableway of ski center Strednica a.s.: 2018.

ŠIŠKA, Dušan. *Director, Ski & Sun Bachledová dolina*: 2017 TUDAJ, Ivan. *Director of the land fund, Poprad*: 2017 VOJTAŠÁKOVÁ, Helena (1949). *Museum – House of Ždiar –Ždiarsky dom*: 2018.

ZORIČÁKOVÁ, Magdaléna (1951). *Museum – House of Ždiar – Ždiarsky dom, former director of the primary school, head of the ensemble Ždiaranček, creator of curriculum for regional education at the primary school*: 2018.

**Contact:**
MA Lucia Kurpašová KMKaT FoA CPU in Nitra Štefánikova 67
949 74 NITRA
E-mail: lucia.kurpasova@ukf.sk

Jana Popovicsová

Department of Slovak Language and Literature, Faculty of
Arts, Constantine the Philosopher University in Nitra

# Searching for the Identity of the Protagonist Blanka in the Works of Ivana Dobrakovová

**Abstract:** In our contribution, we will focus on the personal identity development
of the main protagonists of two works by Ivana Dobrakovová. First, we will interpret the novel *Bellevue* (2010) whose plot takes place in the Institute for Physical
and Mental Disabilities in Marseille, France. The second text will be a short story
*Rosa*, the first story from the collection *Toxo* (2013). In both texts, we will track
the identity evolution of the heroines, whose names are incidentally the same, and
follow the influence environment has on those characters. We will then analyze
how both characters reflect their own self-perception in the context of the story.

**Keywords:** Literature, slovak literature, Ivana Dobrakovová, identity.

The Czech literary historian and critic Michal Jareš described Ivana
Dobrakovová as "the writer who writes about the annoyances and
disorders" (Jareš, 2013, p. 13). We have chosen the work of Ivana
Dobrakovová for several reasons. One of them is her affiliation with
the line of contemporary Slovak female prose-writers, whose works
are a strong and significant component of contemporary Slovak prose.
Contemporary Slovak prose complements the varied nature of contemporary Slovak production with its thematic and formal specifics in authors
such as Monika Kompaníková, Ivan Gibová, Zuska Kepplová, Svetlana
Žuchová, Ursulu Kovalyk and others. The quality of these authors is
exemplified by nominations and victories in prestigious literary contests
like the Anasoft litera, John Johanides Prize, The Short Story and others.

Our interest in the texts of I. Dobrakovová stems from their literary and
aesthetic qualities. I. Dobrakovová is considered not only one of the best
contemporary prose-writers but also a representative of one the most out-
standing phenomena of literary production to appear in the twenty-first
century. In her works (specifically her short-story collections, *The First*

*Death in Family*, *Toxo*, and *Bellevue* novel), she deals exclusively with female protagonists, but does not slip into the schematic portrayal of a woman perpetuating stereotypes. The aim of her work could be considered an attempt to understand femininity, to penetrate into the female psyche, or in essence, to try to understand female identity.

At first glance, women in I. Dobrakovová's texts lead a happy organized family life. However, under the focused attention of the author, they reveal their darkest thoughts and feelings. The main heroine is a complex personality who, under the pressure of external circumstances and classical women's duties, cannot find a balance in herself, and ultimately the power to face the world. I. Dobrakovová's paints all kinds of women – mothers, daughters, girlfriends, pregnant women – against the backdrop of the tiny duties of everyday life. However, Dobrakovová reveals that what goes on inside their psyches is detailed and deep. I. Dobrakovová shows how a lonely and comfortable routine may affect the fragile psyche of a person and how easily the simplest things in life may become the most difficult.

Her works are rich in a sense of alienation accompanied by frequent misunderstandings. The feeling of being misunderstood refers mostly to relationships with men, but also in relations with other female characters (like mother, friend, housemaid). Misunderstanding may come from all sides, regardless of gender, yet at least at the beginning of the story, the protagonists still try to explain their "odd" thoughts and behavior that at some point begin to be influenced by the character's psychological difficulties. People are social creatures. People need to be understood and integrate into the community, and Dobrakovová's protagonist is no exception. At the beginning, Dobrakovová's characteres tend to be understood and accepted, but gradually they realize their efforts are fruitless and their goal is unattainable. The communication barrier between them and others grows bigger and bigger. The characters gradually become isolated and closed, aware of their inability to explain the difficult situation they find themselves in the outside world because of their (real or fabricated) difficulties. At some points, their isolation may also be perceived as voluntary resignation, the simplest way out.

Dobrakovová does not compare men and women in her writings, which we perceive as a positive aspect of her work. The man often plays a minor role and is at least partially and sometimes marginally present in her texts. Dobrakovová does not dive deep into his psyche. In her texts, the man only represents an even composition of a husband, father, breadwinner, friend, partner, and colleague. Through the woman-man relationship, Dobrakovová illustrates the man's inability to understand woman's feeling and way of thinking. She uses the relationship to demonstrate the mutual communication block, or the complete impossibility thereof. The dialogue in her texts transforms into two unrelated monologues disconnected in meaning at the language level and brilliantly served in long sentences, without marking the direct utterances. All of these stylistic nuances are typical for Dobrakovová´s stylistics.

Dobrakovová tends to put stereotypical opinions into the utterances of men, but it is worth noting that the male character sometimes expresses, in a very simple and factual way, the exact reality that a woman can no longer see because of the tangle of confused thoughts and feelings inside her.

> Inwardly emptied, but also craving for understanding; informally overwhelmed, and therefore indifferent or insensitive, but at the same time longing for affection; escaping from one's self to mass consumption and entertainment – these are just a few points that we encounter quite often in attempts to describe a person (Tomašovičová, 2006, p. 165).

What if the fundamental task of being human, i.e. thinking and acting according to established social standards, seems insurmountable? What if we do not identify with the image of femininity that has been produced by postmodern society and the media? When we do not have answers to these questions, doubt, reassessment, anxiety, and depression come into our life; this is exactly the world Dobrakovová leads us through in her works. Her reality is cruel, and her characters end up tragically misunderstood by their closest surroundings, unable to adapt and unable to be human.

*Bellevue* is the work Dobrakovová perceives as her most important book so far. In this work, we observed the personal identity of the main protagonist and interpreted the changes and subsequent disappearance thereof. First of all, the definition of personal identity we use in our work is not definitive, nor generally recognized as valid. Personal identity is a broad concept and can be interpreted from many different perspectives. In this contribution, we deal with the definition of identity by Petra Muráriková (2014). Muráriková is an ethics scientist who, in the publication *The Search for Self*, focuses on the classification and analysis of many kinds of identities, drawing from a large number of available Slovak and foreign sources. The work examines and compares three mutually competing concepts of identity based on three ideological orientations: traditional Christianity, feminism, and new feminism and Muráriková herself leans toward the third type, which seeks to raise up women's specificity.

Muráriková derives the concept of identity as found in new feminism (or feminism of difference) from the theory of Slovak philosopher Ján Letz (1999, 2008). He perceives the concept of identity at three levels. The first level is the concept of personal identity that plays a key role in our contribution. This level is related to the desire for inclusion of one's self into the social context. The second level is related to socialization and the third relates to the image the individual has of himself. Identity is understood to be the identification of one's self with one's self, and against external factors in the case of "holistic identity," wherein the three levels of identity mentioned above are unconditionally related to each other. When considering personal identity, it is necessary to deal with the attributes of identity on the basis of the way in which individual relations and bonds are created (Muráriková, 2014, pp. 20–23). Muráriková concludes that

> identity can be characterized as an inertia in the flow of time, thanks to which a person stays themselves in this flow. It has the character of a stable and supportive point, not of an unchangeable fatality, but an ever-changing spiritually intellectual product. It expresses what is essential to a person, and therefore her search for it is to a great extent a search for the essence of one's self. It is somewhat of a transcendental idea and a regulatory principle, a certain self-image, self-interpretation, an idea of one's self (Muráriková, 2014, p. 24).

In our contribution, we will try to interpret the two texts by I. Dobrakovová that feature the character Blanka, in the light of "the search for one's self." The first case being the novel *Bellevue* (2010) and the latter one being the first short story from the short-story collection *Toxo* (2013), *Rosa*. Our goal is to monitor external and internal influences that condition the transformation of the main character's identity and then analyze the individual.

The novel *Bellevue* describes the story of nineteen-year-old Blanka who decides to spend the summer volunteering at the Bellevue Disabled Facility in Marseilles in southern France. She leaves her home and boyfriend behind to set off toward life's challenge. She seeks to work abroad on her own, improve her skills in the French language, and partake in the joys of summer on the seaside. At the beginning of the novel, we consider her trip to Bellevue a holiday activity common for young adults. We consider her trip an opportunity to gain work habits, practice, and make contacts; all of which make for a normal and productive way to spend summer holiday. However, her trip may also be considered an attempt to find herself. The trip can be seen as a way for Blanka to confirm her own opinion of herself, or rather as an attempt to become a better version of herself, which is obvious from the first few pages of the work. Metaphorically, it is possible to say that Blanka, aware of the limits of her nature, tries to overcome her limits by "throwing herself in at the deep end." However, this experience will not have a positive effect.

Blanka is staying in a volunteer house. There, she meets a Czech girl Martina, who days makes it easier for Blanka to integrate into the group and the work habits in Blanka's first days. Although faced with the usual difficulties of a newcomer, Blanka gradually integrates into the work process. The work consists of caring for people with physical and mental disabilities, most of whom are confined to a wheelchair and are nearly unable to control their body (waking up, morning hygiene, dressing, eating, etc.).

Blanka's inner turmoil is revealed to the reader gradually, only hinted to initially in Blanka's thought processes. It is only later that the inner upset becomes directly manifest through her actions. We soon discover that Blanka has several problems, both with herself and with her surroundings. These problems become apparent on several levels and over time turn into a disaster in the form of a mental illness. We identified that Blanka's conflict exist on four levels: Blanka's relationship to her colleagues, to her work, to the disabled she works with, all of which being realized in the sphere of social identity. Identity influences and directly determines the fourth level, the personal one, which is Blanka's perception of herself. Due to the limited text range, we will deal mostly with the third and fourth levels, i.e. Blanka's relationship to the disabled and the subsequent impact it has on her psyche. In the conclusions, we will briefly outline the first two levels.

We have discovered a developmental arc in Blanka's relationship with the Bellevue residents (as Dobrakovová calls the disabled patients in the institution). Blanka's perceptions of the people suffering from physical disabilities begins as any normal nineteen-year-old person's thinking would and develops into paranoia. The paranoia later develops into psychological illness to such an extent that Blanka loses the ability to control her own body. In other words, we follow an arc going from distinction to identity, wherein the protagonist undergoes six stages of transformation. Her relationship to the respondents develops in a non-standard way and gradually increases until it takes on a pathological character.

The first initial point is that Blanks begins with a normal perception of herself, as a healthy regular woman with adequate ambitions and dreams. This state is present only at the very beginning of the text and after only a few pages the second stage appears: doubt about what is actually normal.

Initially, Blanka perceives herself a healthy person, able to stand and walk on her own two feet. This perception contrast sharply with the wheelchair-bound she encounters. Blanka rightly considers herself happier than the patients, satisfied with her difference from them. Gradually, though, she begins to perceive herself as "deviating from normality" and self-doubt arises. For a full illustration of the unfolding of this phenomenon manifested, see page 16.

In the ordinary world, the disabled are the minority, but in Bellevue institution, the contrary is true. At Bellevue, there are fewer healthy and vital individuals. Blanka's initial nervousness toward this imbalance leads her to perceiving herself as "abnormal," because within Bellevue the rule of "the majority is normal" is switched. This phenomenon is visible in the following extract:

> As I was walking down the corridor out of the building, I met the wheelchair-bound buzzing around … I was walking among them like a giant and looking away inconspicuously, it seemed to me to be inept to stare and also inept to not look at them, by hook or by crook I tried to look natural, as if it was nothing unusual to have no legs, head twice the size of a normal person … I was going further down the corridor when all of a sudden I found it terribly vulgar that I had two legs, and both functional, that I am superiorly strolling among them, I said to myself, do not be absurd, as if it were an insult, immorality, having two legs, or perhaps even guilt, for a moment I almost wished to be like them, to sit in a wheelchair, or at least not to stick out so horribly (pp. 15–16).

The third stage of the arc of Blanka's development is her becoming aware of the possibility that she, a healthy individual, could become just as disabled as the patients she looks after. Blanka starts to gradually approach the other pole of the "distinction–identity" axis. The first sign of a possible development of this identity occurred with Laurence, a resident of a similar age to Blanka. Laurence is severely disabled. In addition to being unable to control her body, Laurence cannot control her facial muscles and is unable to communicate verbally. In one scene, Blanka helps Laurence with her morning hygiene and sees Laurence naked, which makes Blanka realize that there is no real difference between her and the disabled Laurence. Unprepared, this knowledge strikes Blanka at her core. This is the first sign of fear as Blanka realizes it is possible for her healthy body to be as damaged, ill, and disabled as Laurence's.

> I felt awful, literally paralyzed by horror and powerlessness, I only thought of how soon will I scram, her expressions of affection terrified me even more than her expressions of defiance, but the hardest thing for me was to look at those dense curly hairs in her crotch, the necessity to admit that her genitalia look exactly like the genitalia of any other woman, that despite the shrieks and spasms she's still a woman with a vagina between her legs. I could not help myself with the disgust she caused in me, but at the same time I felt a kind of affinity, closeness, a persistent feeling that I could have been like that, if a chance or fate decided so (pp. 25–26).

This idea scares Blanka and from that moment on this paranoid image of herself being the residents haunts her until it becomes reality.

Blanka's identity shift continues to develop as she realizes that the residents themselves are responsible for their disease. Suddenly she finds spiritual perversion and evil coming from within them and understands their disability. Immediately thereafter, this understanding raises a strong wave of joy in her, because she is the good and happy one, not someone determined by a disorder. Blanka finally gains a sense of superiority and self-confidence, something she lacked most her life and the feeling of difference deepens in her – though only for a brief moment.

When Blanka first becomes aware of her similarity to the disabled, she experiences health problems, such as nausea, inability to eat, and vomiting. These symptoms are what we see as further evidence of her transformation. Moreover, she starts directing conversations with other volunteers to morbid topics (suicide, horror movies, she buys a satanic church postcard). Blanka's fear of the possibility that she might become ill gradually grows into nightmares she experiences:

> I lose control over myself at night, sleep cannot be controlled. It's hard to breath in the evening, I cry into the pillow, what if I am not strong enough? … I am terribly afraid that I will piss or shit myself at night, that my body will stop obeying

me, I am terribly afraid ... do you think it would be very stupid if I start putting
a diaper on at night (p. 69)?

These thoughts grow inside her until they consume her whole day, and
finally become reality.

There are many moments that make up the last stage of the development arc. These moments culminate in paranoia and escalated conflicts,
until the situation climaxes and all that Blanka has been afraid of the
whole time becomes true. At first secretly and then openly, Blanka is eventually under the influence of the disease and the roles change. She becomes
the one who is limp and placed in the institution. She becomes a resident
and the transformation from distinct personality to identity becomes final.
She gives up on her body, accepts the situation she has gotten into, and
becomes voluntarily lethargic. At this point, the narrator's point of view
shifts and the narrator depersonalizes himself from the protagonist by
changing the point of view to the second person.

The following quote exemplifies the culmination of Blanka's transformation and narrator's viewpoint shift:

> They touch you, you open your eyes, some people are leaning over you, undress
> you, their sweaty palms, their mechanical movements, their coordination, they
> hold your hands to take off your t-shirt, you let them freely fall back, bang like
> wooden hands of a marionette, you have no strength, no will, no control, you are
> lying naked on the table, ... you are not ashamed of your nakedness, you are not
> proud of it, nothing, a brain shield (p. 170).

We will now briefly mention the first two stages: the relationship with
colleagues and relationship with work. In the process of building
relationships with colleagues, Blanka is initially unable to show interest.
She was jealous of her colleague Martina and unable to express her lack of
interest, evident in her allowing the Romanian woman to show her travel
brochures she is not at all interested in. Blanka is fundamentally aware of
her inability to integrate into the group and perceives the abysmal difference between herself and other the volunteers. The reader may notice the
protagonist's low self-esteem (ego), which manifests itself in trifles, the
inability to be assertive, a communication barrier, and her body language.
However, as Blanka's psyche undergoes a gradual transformation, her
attitude toward others changes in line with the transformation. On the
outside, she starts to act more confidently; her reactions are abrupt and

unexpected. The one who initially did not want to draw attention to herself became the one seeking attention. However, her behavior is obviously insincere, and the question arises as to whether or not she believes in the image she tries to create in front of others. Her faked self-confidence is not long-lasting, and with increasing disease it is subdued and soon disappears completely.

Blanka's relationship to work is similar. It was initially forcefully positive, motivated by her fear of failure. Blank's fear of failure was not a fear of physically injuring patients in the institute. Her concern was actually for her image and how she was being perceived by others. Initially, Blanka's attempts to make a good impression on the new team is obvious. Blanka learns what her job is all about, disgusted by some of her duties related to hygiene. She is relatively clumsy at work. Everything takes too long; residents are dissatisfied with her work and do not cooperate. Blanka gets distressed by every little mistake, any failure, or hostility on the part of patients. At first, she subdues failures and moments of humiliation at work but later confides in the other volunteers. Eventually, she is unable to relax, either by telling her colleagues or crying on the emergency staircase. She later comes to a more radical solution and begins to cut herself and later gives up work completely. Finally, because of her mental illness, she is forced to leave Bellevue and becomes a resident who cannot control her own body.

This finding is directly related to the third stage: a direct relationship with Bellevue residents. It is only in relation to the Bellevue residents that the mental disorder that Blanka succumbs to at the end is fully manifested. Blanka has a problem with self-identification and self-acceptance, not only on the mental but also on the physical level. It is possible to deduce this by how much Blanka keeps defining herself in contrast to the affected residents. Among other things, this is shown in the way she thinks of herself, even in the context of direct interactions with physically handicapped people and in several marginal moments as well, e.g. she only eats an apple for breakfast to avoid gaining weight, she inadequately enjoys a fairly rapid weight loss, and so on. Feelings of nervousness emerge in her consciousness, stemming from her apparent physical oddness in terms of contrast between a healthy and physically disabled, deformed body.

The protagonist's inadequate reflection of the patients is apparent from the beginning of the book, and eventually it forms into pathological dimensions. Blanka is aware that she physically stands out substantially from the disabled residents moving around in wheelchairs and feels the need to blend in with them in an anonymous crowd, where she would not attract any attention to herself (said in her rhetoric, to go down to their level).

There is a perceptible need in her thought processes to make a positive impression on her surroundings in an attempt to achieve an appropriate social status. All of her anxieties are originally based on the fear of what an image of herself can she create in front of unknown colleagues, even if this image does not correspond to reality. She has a very low opinion of herself, and her effort to improve does not stem from the need for self-development, nor does it bring about an internal transformation, it is only directed outward. After all, we can also find remarkable evidence in her utterances in the text in which she expresses her dissatisfaction with her own flesh:

> I am totally convulsive among people, I do not know what to do with the body, as if it didn't belong to me, just a pendant, a burden I have to drag behind me... I hate when someone looks at me ... even now, I walk home from the ward through side streets, so that I do not meet anyone ... I can't bear being physical, I feel ridiculous, with these two hands, legs, torso, though it is absurd, everyone has a body, and mine is no worse than any other ... organs pulsing, heart pumping, stomach digesting, blood circulating, rashes on the face growing, hair getting greasy, breasts bouncing, and I'm not talking about the rest, the body is just a burden... in life (pp. 50–51).

Blanka continually contemplates herself, not only on the levels outlined by us but also in other aspects of life. Critic Miriam Suchánková expressed it as "self-picking, an expression that in the given context cannot be construed otherwise than with a negative connotation (2010, p. 23). Obsessing over one's own problems (both trifles and difficult life situations) and their repeated analysis will eventually lead Blanka to pathological conclusions and personal collapse.

All the above-mentioned situations, which the work is saturated with, evidence Blanka's problematic perception of personality. Furthermore, allusions to the search for one's own identity appear directly in the text. Her friend, Drago, tells her that it seems as if she was running away from herself, as if she was afraid of confrontation. Blanka too, is aware of her search, not just in moments when depression defeats her, but also when she experiences a happy moment. "Is armistice only temporary?" she asks (p. 56). We believe that the most important impetus for the outbreak of a mental illness, which results in the loss of one's own personality, was the direct confrontation with the physically handicapped residents of the Bellevue Institute. There are also other factors in addition to the psychological disorder. It is also the influence of a foreign country, loneliness, clumsiness at work, forming a pathological friendship with her colleague, Luco, and the daily trivialities that her fragile soul infested with the parasitic disease could not withstand.

At the beginning, we notice Blanka's absolute definiteness toward them and the clearly defined difference on the mental and physical level. Gradually, her consciousness is invaded by thoughts that allow for the possibility of identifying with the hated individuals living in Bellevue, until eventually the protagonist begins to admit this possibility. She oscillates between moments in which she is still able to make herself believe that she has enough power to defend herself against the dark forces of her own mind, and moments in which her depression fully breaks out. The following paranoid ideas, multiplied by fear, initially invade her dreams and later also her thoughts throughout the day, taking over her physical body. That is when the turn from difference to identity is completed and Blanka becomes exactly what she feared the most.

If some literary critics evaluate this work as a work dealing with insanity, psychological disintegration (Taranenková, 2010, p. 35), the sensation of flesh and its confrontation (Suchánková, 2010, pp. 21–22), inexplicability, or rather only a seeming, partial explanation of the world (Prušková, 2010, pp. 21–22), about female intimacy (Szentesiová, 2010, p. 1), then we dare to evaluate it as a work dealing with the loss of one's self, losing one's identity.

Dobrakova's next book *Toxo* also includes a stoy about a heroine with the same name. *Toxo* is a collection of short stories that opens with *Rosa*. The main heroine is Blanka, by which Dobrakova indirectly follows the previous novel. It is questionable how likely it is for her to be the same character. This work does not aim to answer this question, but to outline the similarities between the two main protagonists.

The plot of *Rosa* presents the fragments of life of Slovak woman, Blanka, living in Italy. Compared to Blanka from the novel *Bellevue*, Blanka in the opening story of *Toxo* is a grown-up twenty-three-year-old woman who moved to Italy to be with a certain man, which is an occurrence present in the rest of the collection.

In this text, the *Toxo* Blanka also reflects on the flesh, while the object of her interest in this case is the cleaning lady employed by Blanka's who was employed husband and who spends days at their home, lascivious Italian television programs, and unknown Italian women living their everyday life.

While Blanka's partner Luigi is at work, Rosa – after whom the short story has been named – takes care of all aspects of the household. She cleans, goes shopping, and cooks while being accompanied by the constantly silent Slovak woman. Rosa fulfils the role of a housewife and Blanka, who is unemployed, loses her daylong pastime. At first, Blanka tries to get involved in housework, but neither Rosa nor Luigi consider her capable enough of carrying out basic household chores. Hints appear in the text that she is considered incapable because of her Slovak origin. Under the pressure of circumstances, Blanka submits to the routine. Rosa has been taking care of Luigi's apartment for years and has her own system and becomes more or less an observer of a woman in whom she begins to identify her exact opposite.

A difference also forms on several levels of the text, including Rosa's open attitude toward Blanka. Rosa does not respect Blanka, because the protagonist comes from a country in Eastern Europe, whereas Rosa believes polygamy is still possible, men have genetic predispositions to rape and kill women, war still exists along with poverty and misery, and order and cleanliness are not maintained at home. The fact that she is a Slovak woman makes her an unusual thing in the eyes of the Italian, a fact that she reminds Blanka every day in various ways. This is exemplified by the fact that Rosa addresses Blanka every day by a different name, undermining not only Blanka's authority in the household but also her self-awareness. Already at this point in the text, Blanka's belief in her own inferiority is implied.

While Blanka is quiet, non-conflicting and appreciates her private, intimate space, Rosa acts as the opposite elemental type of woman. During the day she constantly talks about herself and her private life, commenting openly on the social situation in the country and she does not avoid even criticizing the country which Blanka comes from, e.g. in the extract: "and has war been in your country for a long time? Blanka is puzzled, 'War? There is no war in my country.' Rosa is silent, then, somewhat more decisively, says 'but hunger and cold and poverty, you have it, you cannot deny that.' Blanka does not deny" (p. 13).

Consideration of the feminine physicality is also reflected in this of I. Dobrakovová's text, when Blanka perceives the maid, Rosa, as "corpulent" (p. 8). She is substantially aware of the space that Rosa fills with her body and how her activity begins to expand into an ever-increasing space, usurping more and more of Blanka's immediate surroundings. A feeling grows in Blanka that Rosa is reducing her living space with her body, interfering in her privacy. Rosa does it not only thuruogh her physical presence but also through the constant noisy presence, usurping of truth and opinions, or by how well she gets on with Luigi.

Rosa's penetration into Blanka's space was also physically evident by continuous touching with warm, wet hands. Blanka is not able to protest against such a behavior, which in her perception is an almost aggressive invasion of her privacy. Blanka is unable to express her opinion clearly and instead suffers silently. Initially, Blanka tries to explain her problem to her partner, but he does not attach importance to it. He considers the complaint to be unimportant and does not support her in any way. This confirms the tendency of I. Dobrakovová's characters, which we outlined at the beginning of this paper as we see at least a partial, initial effort to solve the problem that nevertheless remains without response and therefore the heroine gives up and closes herself off.

The need for privacy and the need for one's own space, as is customary in the Dobrakova's protagonists, results in an anxious behavior on behalf of the heroine. Blanka cannot bear the idea that Rosa would find a used condom in the garbage bin, let alone touch it. She is not able to eat in front of her, nor appear before Rose in her pajamas. Every day, Blanka gets up half an hour before her arrival to make basic morning hygiene and eat breakfast. Her way of defending herself is turning inward, which is again a feature that appears in several Dobrakova's works.

Moreover, the need for privacy manifests itself in Blanka's general inability to consume food in the presence of another person, a parallel with Blanka from *Bellevue*, whose problematic consumption was based on fear of weight gain. Blanka elevates public consumption to one of the biggest problems of her life, which is reflected in her relationship with her husband and Rosa. She feels physical repulsion at eating, even while doing so by herself, worrying about the possible inability to adjust the correct movements of her mouth and hands. We can see this in the following quote: "reach for a glass of mineral water? send one's hand so far away from the body? after all she must keep her hand close, safe" (p. 20). Both texts coincide in this parallel self-distrust of the protagonist and the effort not to expose herself to public criticism. Furthermore, in this text, she is also aware of her inability to express her feelings to her husband for fear that he will consider her inferior.

Unlike in *Bellevue*, Blanka from *Rosa* reflects her own femininity, or more precisely its absence, far more noticeably. In the novel, the mutual sexual characteristics between her and the physically handicapped resident of Bellevue admitted the possibility that she too could become equally disadvantaged. However, in *Rosa*, Blanka's attention focused on the feminine more notably. In the latter text, even at twenty-three, Blanka has a problem with her appearance, which causes unpleasant moments (in the restaurant when serving wine or in the screening of films suitable for adult viewers) as she perceives Italian women as naturally more feminine, which is not primarily because of their facial features, makeup, or clothing, but for something immaterial that cannot be captured. Something in the way they walk, move, and express themselves. According to the principle of identity-difference, Blanka begins to define herself even in contrast to them in a negative sense, considering herself as inferior, less feminine. The the feeling of difference is the strongest in the street, where she is confronted with Italian women face-to-face, outside her private safe space.

One of the most striking levels in this case is the level of the physical body, which though similar in *Bellevue*, has a different shape in the short story. While in Bellevue it was a healthy opposition, the opposition of not being afflicted with disease, in this text it is femininity itself and Italian beauty contrasted with being insufficiently feminine and Slovak. This is reflected in utterances by Rosa, who often reminds her of the plump beauty of her daughters, describing Italian women returning home from shopping and stars from television programs, who themselves are a showcase of perfectly feminine bodies. The insolent sexuality presented in the media, which Blanka initially resented, leads her to the realization that it is natural, and her perception is wrong.

Similar to *Bellevue*, Blanka suffers day to day and the suffering is projected into her dreams. She dreams of an overexposed sexual situation; the basis of which is obviously her everyday experiences with housemaid Rosa. Blanka finds Rosa's body disgusting all the more, because Rosa forces her to touch it: "In a few months, Blanka got to know all the bruises, burns, abrasions, scars, birthmarks, warts, she could admire, evaluate, feel, Rosa wasn't sparing of her body, Rosa was handing it round, Rosa wanted to share her body with everyone" (p. 32). These two women are totally different in their perception of their own bodies. While one of them is proud and flaunts her body, not only directly but also subconsciously in demonstrative movements, the other constantly shames her body and compares it against the media images of Italian women.

A key moment in the story is Blanka's memory of an erotic dream in which there is a sexual connection with one of her female high school classmates. Immediately, Blanka recalls the first experience with gynecological examination, which was very unpleasant for her. "Blanka is moving on the examination table, she closes herself, literally, the doctor is swearing, come down, where are you climbing? Relax, Blanka is crying, Blanka is convinced at the moment that she suffers from vaginism, that someone is just raping her in a dark park" (p. 36).

Ever since that dream, she envisions Rosa in the apartment even when Rosa is not physically present. Her image keeps coming back to Blanka in a paranoid manner and she is unable to defend herself. Thoughts of her became a part of her everyday life including eating, hygiene, and sexual intercourse with Luigi. Initially, we see Blanka's efforts to resist these thoughts. For example, when making love with her husband, she imagines "everything, anything, vegetables and fruits she buys on the market, what exactly she needs, the shape of the pepper, the color, and also the pears, the giant ones that have a wax-covered stem..." (pp. 38–39). Blanka's efforts to not succumb to panic and anxiety attacks culminate when Rosa touches her naked breasts to discuss the need to undergo surgery to improve them. At that moment Blanka awakens, observes herself from a distance, from outside of her body, and immediately runs away from the apartment and flees the country to go back to her hometown.

The possible reason for her escape is found in the final part of the last sentence of the short story: "Blanka does not hope for another man" (p. 42). This is Blanka clearly expressing what has not been indicated in the text until now: Blanka doubts her sexual orientation. Her escape may foreshadow the fear of identification, as we have pinpointed in the previous novel. While Blanka from *Bellevue* collapsed mentally and physically, Blanka from *Rosa* flees before she can fully realize her newly discovered identity and succumb to its consequences. Her escape evokes a long-term absence of self-knowledge that has been challenged by fear of her own sexuality.

Even her initial resistance to Rosa's older body may be understood as fear of sexuality in general and fear of her own sexuality. There are some indications in the text that could lead the reader to believe that Blanka is homosexual. However, in our opinion it is rather a concern about such a possibility, because it is the fear of the first hint of a problem that tends to be hyperbolized into extreme situations in Dobrakovová's texts.

In terms of the observed topic, this text is an attempt to protect the main protagonist's inner self from the invasion on the part of the housemaid Rosa – even though Rosa is unaware of the invasion. It is typical of Dobrakovová's main protagonists to experience situations much more sensitively than expected, exceed the reality with their imagination. Dobrakovová's characters are loners who do not have the ability to express their feelings and fears in a way that can be understood by their partners, friends, or family. This causes them to gradually grow apart from everyone else and turn inwards and constantly doubt and re-evaluate their inner life.

## Conclusions

In our paper we dealt with two texts by the Slovak author Ivana Dobrakovová: the novel debut *Bellevue* and the story *Rosa* from the collection of short stories, *Toxo*. Both texts are connected by the presence of the main heroine Blanka, who may be defined as mentally unstable, searching for herself, searching for her identity. In this sense, the identity of a person is understood as an expression of what is essential to them and therefore their search is largely a search for the essence of himself / herself.

In both texts we analyzed the development, or rather the transformation of, the psyche of this character. This transformation, which takes place under the influence of external stimuli and on the principle of identicalness-difference, is theoretically defined by P. Muráriková in her scientific work. At one point, the heroine begins to experience the problems of this opposition firsthand and tries to deal with it by defining herself. She starts with an attempt to define herself against a difference that she finds in her neighborhood. While Blanka from *Bellevue* faced an opposition of healthy versus affected by a disease, Blanka from *Rosa* felt the opposition of feminine, beautiful, Italian versus insufficiently pretty, insufficiently feminine, Slovak.

In both cases the fear of identification was the driving force of this psychic transformation of self-perception. It is the fear itself that is the first indication of a problem, which then tends to be hyperbolized into extreme situations in Dobrakovová's texts. The heroines in both texts went through an evolutionary arc from difference to sameness, which was realized through various impulses that connected physical corporeality, dissatisfaction on both the physical and the mental levels, and the presence of unpleasant external entities mainly in the form of specific characters (residents in the novel Bellevue and Italian women and Rosa in the story Rosa).

The culmination of both texts is the personality collapse of the main protagonist. While Blanka from *Bellevue* reached a critical state in the form of a personality collapse on both psychological and physical levels, Blanka from *Rosa* ran away from identifying with her sexuality. The escape in this case may be perhaps explained as an unwillingness to know and accept herself. The remaining question is, what would happen to Blanka later on if the texts were real life stories?

# References:

BUTLER, J. 2015. *Trampoty s rodom: feminizmus a podrývanie identity*. Bratislava: Záujmové združenie žien Aspekt, 2014, p. 268. ISBN 978-80-8151-028-1.

CSIBA, K. a kol. 2014. *Hľadanie súčasnosti: slovenská literatúra začiatku 21. storočia*. Bratislava: Literárne informačné centrum, p. 219. ISBN 978-80-8119-085-8.

DOBRAKOVOVÁ, I. 2009. *Prvá smrť v rodine*. Bratislava: Marenčin PT, p. 192. ISBN 978-80-8114-007-5.

DOBRAKOVOVÁ, I. 2010. *Bellevue*. Bratislava: Marenčin PT, p. 240. ISBN 978-80-8114-030-3.

DOBRAKOVOVÁ, I. 2014. *Toxo*. Bratislava: Marenčin PT, p. 192. ISBN 978-80-8114-189-8.

JAREŠ, M. 2013. O matkách a dětech. In *Romboid*. ISSN 0231-6714. 2013, roč. 48, č. 9, pp. 13–18.

KARPINSKÝ, P. 2011. *Päť x päť. Antológia súčasnej slovenskej prózy*. Bratislava: Literárne informačné centrum, p. 250. ISBN 978-80-8119-040-7.

LETZ, J. 2008. Naliehavá potreba celostnej identity súčasného človeka. In *Problémy personálnej sebaidentifikácie v súčasnej kultúre*. Trnava: Trnavská univerzita, 1999. ISBN 80-887-463-2. pp. 105–113.

LETZ, J. 2008. Otázka personálnej sebaidentifikácie človeka v súčasnej dobe. In *Identita a identifikácia z pohľadu etiky a morálnej filozofie*. Trnava: Trnavská univerzita, 2008. ISBN 978-80-8082-187-6. pp. 16–33.

MURÁRIKOVÁ, P. 2014. *Hľadanie seba samej : otázka identity ženy v súčasnosti*. Bratislava: IRIS, p. 168. ISBN 978-0-8153-009-8.

PRUŠKOVÁ, Z. 2010. "Bellevue beletria" – biograficky, diskurzívne, pútavo. In *Romboid*. ISSN 0231-6714. 2010, roč. 45. č. 9, pp. 19–24.

SUCHÁNKOVÁ, M. 2010. Román ako vyplnenie ruptúr. In *Romboid*. ISSN 0231-6714. 2010, roč. 45. č. 9, pp. 19–24.

SZENTESIOVÁ, L. 2010. Bellevue. In *Knižná revue*. ISSN 1210-1982. 2010, roč. 20, č. 24, p. 1.

TOMAŠOVIČOVÁ, J. 2006. Zápas o identitu človeka. In *Ľudská prirodzenosť a kultúrna identita*. Bratislava: IRIS. ISBN 80–89238–04–1. pp. 165–186.

http://inaque.sk/sk/clanky/books/fiction/predtucha_niecoho_zleho.

https://kultura.sme.sk/c/7308231/nepotrebujem-vydat-knihu-kazdy-rok. html.

http://filmpiatalod.sk/.

## Studies in Politics, Security and Society

Edited by Stanisław Sulowski

www.peterlang.com